GREEK WORD ORDER

GREEK WORD ORDER

BY

K. J. DOVER

Professor of Greek in the University of St Andrews

CAMBRIDGE

AT THE UNIVERSITY PRESS

1960

CAMBRIDGE UNIVERSITY PRESS
Cambridge, New York, Melbourne, Madrid, Cape Town, Singapore,
São Paulo, Delhi, Dubai, Tokyo

Cambridge University Press
The Edinburgh Building, Cambridge CB2 8RU, UK

Published in the United States of America by Cambridge University Press, New York

www.cambridge.org
Information on this title: www.cambridge.org/9780521134705

First published 1960
This digitally printed version 2010

A catalogue record for this publication is available from the British Library

ISBN 978-0-521-04852-1 Hardback
ISBN 978-0-521-13470-5 Paperback

PREFACE

The essential argument of this book is that of the J. H. Gray Lectures which I gave in Cambridge in February 1959, and I am very greatly indebted to the Board of the Faculty of Classics in Cambridge for giving me the opportunity and encouragement to put into coherent form the results of ten years of intermittent work on the problems of Greek word order. Since the requirements of a reader are not those of a hearer, the original lectures have been reduced by the compression of explanatory passages, expanded by the inclusion of statistics and bibliographical references, and changed in arrangement by the deferment of 'Logical Determinants' to a later part of the book.

I have not attempted a complete historical description of the phenomena of Greek word order, but only the isolation and illustration of what seem to me the most important determinants of order in early Greek prose. The Classical scholar may think my methods and language tainted by the jargon of modern linguistics; the modern linguist may think them the naive dabbling of an old-fashioned Classic in something which he does not understand. Provided the fire from both sides is of roughly equal intensity, I shall have some cause for satisfaction. I believe that students of any language should be receptive to ideas which come from the students of any other language; but I believe at the same time that no language should be described and analysed except in the terms which are positively suggested by its own peculiar nature and the nature of our knowledge of it.

Although there is, I think, much in this book which has not been said before, or not said in the same connections, I have never, in anything that I have written, been so continuously conscious that whatever good there may be in it has been reached by standing on the shoulders of others. I hope that someone will stand on mine as soon as possible, and that I can take the weight. My first stimulus to the study of Greek word order was provided, within a week of my starting work as a Tutor, by Mr R. G. M. Nisbet, who was courteously but firmly unconvinced by a change in order which I wanted to make in a Greek sentence which he had written. Among published works, I have long been indebted to Wackernagel's

'Über ein Gesetz der indogermanischen Wortstellung', Fraenkel's 'Kolon und Satz', Frisk's *Studien zur griechischen Wortstellung*, and Loepfe's *Wortstellung im griechischen Sprechsatz*. Their influence on my argument will be clear enough, I hope, to take the sting out of my criticisms of details in their work. Very many colleagues and friends have helped me by suggestions, criticisms and references, and I thank them all.

K. J. D.

UNIVERSITY OF ST ANDREWS
May 1959

CONTENTS

BIBLIOGRAPHY

The abbreviations of periodicals are those of *L'Année Philologique.*

Bibliographies of Greek word order are given by Schwyzer (*Grammatik*), Schwentner in *W & S* VIII (1923), pp. 179 ff., IX (1924), pp. 194 f., N.F. I (1938), pp. 160 ff., and Maurer, *ibid.* IX (1924), pp. 195 f. These include references to works of the early and middle nineteenth century. Some modern work is briefly mentioned by Schwyzer in *JAW* CC (1924), pp. 138 ff., and Risch, *Gl* XXXV (1956), pp. 33 ff. There is a good bibliography of general linguistic works in Sandmann (see below). The articles of Firbas (see below) contain many references to work on individual modern languages, including work in and on Slavonic languages.

The works listed in the following bibliography are referred to in my footnotes (i) by the author's name only, if the author appears only once in the bibliography, (ii) by the author's name and an abbreviation of the title, if the author is represented by more than one work.

I mark * those works which seem to me to be of exceptional value to the student of Greek word order.

AMMANN, H. 'Die Stellungstypen des lateinischen attributiven Adjectivum und ihre Bedeutung für die Psychologie der Wortstellung auf Grund von Ciceros Briefen an Atticus', *IF* XXIX (1911/12), pp. 1 ff.

—— 'Vom doppelten Sinn', *SHAW* (ph.-hist.) 1920, no. 12.

*—— *Untersuchungen zur homerischen Wortfolge und Satzstruktur*, I, Freiburg i. B., 1922.

*—— 'Untersuchungen, etc', II, *IF* XLII (1924), pp. 149 ff., 300 ff.

—— 'Wortstellung und Stilentwickelung', *Gl* XII (1923), pp. 107 ff.

BACHHAMMER, F. *Die Spaltung eng verbundenen Wörter bei Thukydides*, Diss. Erlangen, 1921.

BARBELENET, D. *De la phrase à verbe 'être' dans l'ionien d'Hérodote*, Paris, 1913.

—— 'Sur la place de γίνομαι dans la phrase d'Hérodote', *MSL* XIX (1914), pp. 105 ff.

BARTH, P. 'Zur Psychologie der gebundenen und der freien Wortstellung', *Philosophische Studien* XXIX (=*Festschrift Wilhelm Wundt*), pp. 22 ff.

BEHAGHEL, O. 'Beziehungen zwischen Umfang und Reihefolge von Satzgliedern', *IF* XXV (1909), pp. 110 ff.

—— 'Zur Stellung des Verbs im Germanischen und Indogermanischen', *ZVS* LVI (1929), pp. 276 ff.

BERGAIGNE, A. 'Essai sur la construction grammaticale', *MSL* III (1878), pp. 1 ff., 124 ff., 169 ff. [Left incomplete by author's death.]

BISHOP, C. E. 'The Greek Verbal in -TEO', III, *AJPh* XX (1899), pp. 241 ff.

BLOCH, A. 'Über die Entwicklung der Ausdrucksfähigkeit in den Sprachen des Altertums', *MH* I (1944), pp. 234ff.

BLOOMFIELD, M. 'On the variable position of the verb in oldest Sanskrit', *IF* XXXI (1912/13), pp. 156ff.

BOLDT, H. *De liberiore linguae graecae et latinae collocatione verborum capita selecta*, Diss. Göttingen, 1884.

*BOLINGER, D. L. 'Linear Modification', *PMLA* LXVII (1952), pp. 1117ff.

BRUGMANN, K. *Kurze vergleichende Grammatik der indogermanischen Sprachen*, Leipzig, 1904.

—— 'Verschiedenheiten der Satzgestaltung nach Massgabe der seelischen Grundfunktionen in den indogermanischen Sprachen', *BSG* (ph.-hist.) LXX (1918), no. 6.

CHANTRAINE, P. 'Les recherches sur l'ordre des mots en grec', *AFC* V (1952), pp. 71ff.

DELBRÜCK, B. *Die altindische Wortfolge* (=*Syntaktische Forschungen* III), Halle, 1878.

—— *Vergleichende Syntax der indogermanischen Sprachen* III, Strassburg, 1900.

—— 'Germanische Syntax II: Zur Stellung des Verbums', *ASG* (ph.-hist.) XXVIII (1911), Nr. 7.

DENNISTON, J. D. *Greek Prose Style*, Oxford, 1952.

—— *The Greek Particles*, 2nd ed., Oxford, 1954.

DITTMAR, A. *Syntaktische Grundfragen*, Grimma, 1911.

EBELING, H. L. 'Some Statistics on the Order of Words in Greek', *Studies in Honor of Basil L. Gildersleeve* (Baltimore, 1902), pp. 229ff.

ENTWISTLE, W. J. *Aspects of Language*, London, 1953.

FIRBAS, J. 'Thoughts on the Communicative Function of the Verb in English, German and Czech', *Brno Studies in English* I (1959), pp. 39ff.

*—— 'Some Thoughts on the Function of Word Order in Old English and Modern English', *Zvláštní Otisk z Časopisu, Sborník Prací Filos. Fak. Brn. Univ.*, 1957, pp. 72ff.

—— 'On the problem of Non-Thematic Subjects in Contemporary English', Zvláštní otisk: Časopis pro moderni filologii, XXXIX, pp. 22ff., 166ff. [In Czech, with English summary.]

FISCHER, P. 'Zur Stellung des Verbums im Griechischen', *Gl* XIII (1924), pp. 1ff., 189ff.

FRAENKEL, EDUARD. *Iktus und Accent im lateinischen Sprechvers*, Berlin, 1928.

*—— 'Kolon und Satz: Beobachtungen zur Gliederung des antiken Satzes', *NGG* (ph.-hist.) 1932, pp. 197ff., 1933, pp. 319ff.

*FRISK, H. *Studien zur griechischen Wortstellung*, Göteborg, 1933.

VON DER GABELENTZ, G. 'Ideen zu einer vergleichenden Syntax', *ZVPs* VI (1869), pp. 376ff.

VON DER GABELENTZ, G. 'Weiteres zur vergleichenden Syntax', *ZVPs* VIII (1875), pp. 129 ff., 300 ff.
—— *Die Sprachwissenschaft*, 2nd ed., Leipzig, 1901.
GARDINER, A. H. *Speech and Language*, Oxford, 1932.
*GOODELL, T. D. 'The Order of Words in Greek', *TAPhA* XXI (1890), pp. 5 ff.
HATCHER, ANNA G. 'Syntax and the Sentence', *Word* XII (1956), pp. 224 ff.
HAUPT, MORITZ. *Opuscula* II, Leipzig, 1876.
HAVERS, W. 'Zur "Spaltung" des Genetivs im Griechischen', *IF* XXXI (1912/13), pp. 230 ff.
—— *Handbuch der erklärenden Syntax*, Heidelberg, 1931.
HERMANN, E. 'Gab es im Indogermanischen Nebensätze?', *KZ* XXXIII (1894), pp. 481 ff.
HIRT, H. *Indogermanische Grammatik* VII, Heidelberg, 1937.
HOLWERDA, A. E. J. *Specimen literarum continens disputationem de dispositione verborum in lingua graeca, in lingua latina, et apud Plutarchum*, Utrecht, 1878.
JACOBSOHN, H. 'Tagen baren Löneborger Kind', *ZVS* LIV (1927), pp. 100 ff.
—— 'Zum homerischen ὕστερον πρότερον', *ZVS* LVI (1929), pp. 1 ff.
KAIBEL, G. *Stil und Text der* πολιτεία Ἀθηναίων *des Aristoteles*, Berlin, 1893.
KENT, R. G. *Old Persian*, 2nd ed., New Haven, 1953.
*KIECKERS, E. *Die Stellung des Verbs im Griechischen und in den verwandten Sprachen*, Strassburg, 1911.
—— 'Die Stellung der Verba des Sagens in Schaltesätzen im Griechischen und in den verwandten Sprachen', *IF* XXX (1912), pp. 145 ff.
—— 'Zur oratio recta in den indogermanischen Sprachen', I, *IF* XXXV (1915), pp. 1 ff.; II, *IF* XXXVI (1916), pp. 1 ff.
KRAUSE, W. 'Die Entwicklung einer alten elliptischen Konstruktion in den indogermanischen Sprachen', *ZVS* LII (1924), pp. 223 ff.
KÜHNER, R. *Ausführliche Grammatik der griechischen Sprache: Zweiter Teil: Satzlehre*, revised by GERTH, B., 2 vols., Hanover and Leipzig, 1898–1904.
LEO, F. 'Bemerkungen über Plautinische Wortstellung und Wortgruppen', *NGG* (ph.-hist.) 1895, pp. 415 ff.
LEUMANN, M. and HOFMANN, J. B. *Lateinische Grammatik*, Munich, 1928.
*LINDHAMER, LUISE. *Zur Wortstellung im Griechischen*, Diss. Munich, 1908.
*LOEPFE, A. *Die Wortstellung im griechischen Sprechsatz*, Diss. Freiburg i. d. Schw., 1940.
McDONALD, W. H. 'Linguistic Examination of an Epigraphic Formula', *AJA* LIX (1955), pp. 151 ff.

MACDONELL, A. A. *Vedic Grammar*, Oxford, 1916.
MAROUZEAU, J. *L'ordre des mots dans la phrase latine*, 3 vols., Paris, 1922–49.
—— *L'ordre des mots en latin*, Paris, 1953.
MEILLET, A. *Introduction à l'étude comparative des langues indo-européennes*, 7th ed., Paris, 1934.
MEISTER, K. 'Der syntaktische Gebrauch des Genetivs in den kretischen Dialektinschriften', *IF* XVIII (1905/6), pp. 133 ff.
MILDEN, A. W. *The Limitations of the Predicative Position in Greek*, Diss. Baltimore, 1900.
MÜLLER, R. 'De attributo titulorum s. V Atticorum observationes quaedam', *Ph* LXIV (1905), pp. 554 ff.
NEHRBASS, R. *Sprache und Stil der Iamata von Epidauros*, = *Ph* Supplbd. XXVII (1935), no. 4.
PANTAZES, M. Τὸ διασαφητικὸν τῆς ἑλληνικῆς γλώσσης, 'Αθηνᾶ XI (1899), pp. 443 ff.
PAUL, H. *Principien der Sprachgeschichte*, 2nd ed., Halle, 1886.
PITTMAN, R. S. 'Nuclear Structures in Modern Linguistics', *Language* XXIV (1948), pp. 287 ff.
PORZIG, W. Review of AMMANN, *Untersuchungen* I, *IF* XLIV (1927), pp. 94 ff.
POSTGATE, J. P. 'Flaws in Classical Research', *PBA* 1907–8, pp. 161 ff.
RADERMACHER, L. 'Griechischer Sprachgebrauch VII–XIV', *Ph* LXIII (1904), pp. 1 ff.
*RASS, H. J. *Der Satzanbau: Untersuchung über eine eigentümliche Wortstellung im griechischen und im lateinischen*, Diss. Göttingen, 1950. [Typescript.]
*RICHTER, ELISE. 'Grundlinien der Wortstellungslehre', *ZRPh* XL (1920), pp. 9 ff.
ROBERTS, W. RHYS. 'A Point of Greek and Latin Word Order', *CR* XXVI (1912), pp. 177 ff.
*SANDMANN, M. *Subject and Predicate*, Edinburgh, 1954.
SCHICK, CARLA. 'La lingua delle iscrizioni', *RF* N.S. XXXIII (1955), pp. 361 ff.
SCHÖNE, H. 'Verschränkung von Redegliedern im wiedererzählten Dialog', *RhM* LIV (1899), pp. 633 ff.
—— 'Verschiedenes', *RhM* LXXIII (1920–4), pp. 137 ff.
*—— 'Eine umstrittene Wortstellung des griechischen', *H* LX (1925), pp. 144 ff.
SCHULZE, W. 'Eine eigentümliche Wortstellung', *ZVS* LIV (1927), pp. 301 ff.
SCHWYZER, E. *Griechische Grammatik* II (completed by DEBRUNNER, A.), Munich, 1940.
SPIEGEL, F. *Vergleichende Grammatik der altérânischen Sprachen*, Leipzig, 1882.

SPITZER, L. 'Nachtrag zu *Singen und Sagen*', *ZVS* LIV (1927), p. 311.
*THOMSON, G. 'The Postponement of Interrogatives in Attic Drama', *CQ* XXXIII (1939), pp. 147 ff.
THUMB, A. 'Experimentelle Psychologie und Sprachwissenschaft', *GRMS* III (1911), pp. 1 ff., 65 ff.
VAHLEN, J. 'Über zwei Briefe des Alciphron', *SPAW* 1908, pp. 990 ff.
VENDRYES, J. *Le langage*, revised ed., Paris, 1950.
*DE VRIES, J. *Untersuchungen über die Sperrung von Substantiv und Attribut in der Sprache der attischen Redner*, Diss. Freiburg i. B., 1938.
*WACKERNAGEL, J. 'Über ein Gesetz der indogermanischen Wortstellung', *IF* I (1892), pp. 333 ff. (= *Kleine Schriften* I, Göttingen, 1953, pp. 1 ff.).
—— *Über einige antike Anredeformen*, Göttingen, 1912.
—— 'Zur Wortfolge, besonders bei den Zahlwörtern', *Festschrift Gustav Binz*, Basle, 1935, pp. 33 ff. (= *Kl. Schr.* I, pp. 236 ff.).
—— 'Eine Wortstellungsregel des Pāṇini und Wincklers Aleph-Beth Regel', *IF* LVI (1938), pp. 161 ff. (= *Kl. Schr.* I, pp. 434 ff.).
—— 'Indogermanische Dichtersprache', *Ph* XCV (1942), pp. 1 ff.
*WEIL, H. *De l'ordre des mots dans les langues anciennes comparées aux langues modernes*, 3rd ed., Paris, 1879.
WILHELM, A. 'Neue Beiträge zur griechischen Inschriftenkunde', VI, *SAWW* CLXXXIII (1921), no. 3.
—— 'Zur Syntax des griechischen', *NGG* (ph.-hist.) N.F. III (1938), pp. 118 ff.
WUNDT, W. *Völkerpsychologie I. Die Sprache*, 2 vols., Leipzig, 1900.

CHAPTER I

THE NATURE OF THE PROBLEM

(i) INDETERMINACY

The problem of Greek word order is so seldom discussed in this country that it is still possible to treat it as a fresh problem. In this respect it differs from all other problems of comparable magnitude in the study of the Greek language. Of the work so far published on Greek word order, much is cautious and limited in scope, confining itself to the minute analysis of a small number of particular phenomena. Work which aims more ambitiously at a high level of generalisation has borne little fruit. Sometimes this is because the 'rules' which it offers prove inadequate, or break down, as soon as one tries to apply them to a page of Greek in a text opened at random.[1] Sometimes the rules admit neither of proof nor of disproof, because the arguments on which they rest are circular.[2] More often, an objective general statement of the facts appears, to the seeker after rules, inconclusive in the extreme; it amounts to saying '*xyz* and *xzy* occur, but, on the other hand, *yxz*, *yzx*, *zxy*, and *zyx* also occur.' General accounts of word order of the kind which we find in Schwyzer's grammar would have delighted Sextus Empiricus.

It may be argued that if attempts to establish general rules have ended in doubt and confusion, that is the fault not of the enquirers after the truth but of the truth itself, Greek word order being 'free', 'arbitrary' or 'indeterminate'. I do not suggest that such a view is unscholarly or disreputable. It speaks, after all, with the voice of experience and can draw upon a superabundance of evidence. We find an Attic boundary-stone which proclaims itself (*IG*, I², 877) [*h*ο]δõ *h*ó[ρ]oς; we find another, of the same date, which says (*ibid.* 878) *h*ó[ρoς] *h*oδõ. The beginning of chapter 8 of the Hippocratic

[1] Thumb, p. 2, has no difficulty in disposing, by this test, of Kühner's general rule (II, p. 595), but the rule which he substitutes ('middle' position of the verb) can be disposed of with equal ease.

[2] See especially ch. IV, A (i) below (p. 32). Similar criticisms of circularity may be brought against, e.g., Ammann's attempt (*WSt*) to represent differences of Greek order by stylistic differences in translation and Richter's treatment (p. 24) of 'Rhythmuslinien'.

work *De Carne* is τὸ δὲ ἧπαρ ὧδε ξυνέστη; the next chapter begins ὁ δὲ σπλὴν ξυνέστη ὧδε.

Discouraging as such examples may be, we should regard them as opening the question, not as closing it. They suffice to show that there must be *some* degree of indeterminacy in Greek word order; that is to say, it must sometimes be determined by processes in the mind of the composer, rational or irrational, which we cannot necessarily expect to recover. On the other hand, there are very many utterances in Greek which conform to one or other of a limited number of patterns.[1] Take, for example, a complete utterance consisting of the three words πάντα ἂν ἔγραψεν. Mathematically, there are six possible ways of arranging three unlike objects; but out of the six possibilities in this utterance, the majority can be discarded:

(i) ἂν πάντα ἔγραψεν, (ii) ἂν ἔγραψε πάντα. No competent student would write either of these; and any competent student should be able to say why, namely that ἄν never begins a sentence.

(iii) ἔγραψε πάντ' ἄν. Nor, I hope, would a student write this; but I should be surprised if he could say why, except to say (truly) that if we search for an example, in Classical Greek prose, of verb +πάντα+ἄν arranged, as a complete utterance, in this order, our search will be long. All of us, teachers and students alike, constantly avoid abnormal formulations without knowing why, and there is nothing strange in that; the process is comparable with the familiar experience of carrying out a manual operation rightly when we do not attend to it too closely and wrongly when we do.

(iv) πάντ' ἔγραψεν ἄν. This is described by Demetrius, *Eloc.* 256, as a κακόφωνον deviation from πάντα ἂν ἔγραψεν, but something which one might say or write in order to achieve δεινότης; he mentions it with παρεγένετο οὐχί=οὐ παρεγένετο.

(v) ἔγραψεν ἂν πάντα and (vi) πάντ' ἂν ἔγραψεν. On these two alternatives it is enough for the moment to remark that it is (vi), not (v), which Demetrius treats as the norm from which πάντ' ἔγραψεν ἄν is a deviation, and (vi) which we should be more likely to write in a prose composition; reasons for this will be given later.

If it is objected that an example containing a word like ἄν is not a fair example, it is legitimate to answer: what *is* a word 'like ἄν', and which words are 'like ἄν'? And where does the boundary lie

[1] Cf. Vendryes, p. 167.

between the comparative rigidity of πάντ' ἂν ἔγραψεν and the total laxity of ὅρος ὁδοῦ / ὁδοῦ ὅρος?

The purpose of this book is to discover the nature of the principles which would justify us in calling πάντ' ἂν ἔγραψεν 'normal' or 'right' in order.

(ii) TYPES OF DETERMINANT

The respects in which two utterances may be similar or dissimilar are clearly very numerous. If two utterances are syntactically identical, but differ in order, this does not prove that the determinants of their different orders are unknowable; it proves only that syntactical identity does not suffice to determine identity of order; and our task becomes the exploration of all the respects in which the two utterances are dissimilar, in the hope of finding there the vital difference which determined their difference of order.

Let us now take a very simple Greek utterance, the words with which Hippocrates excitedly awakens Socrates at the beginning of Plato's *Protagoras* (310B): Πρωταγόρας ἥκει.[1] Let us discard any beliefs which we may previously have entertained on the determination of word order, and ask in complete innocence: Why, in this particular utterance, does the word Πρωταγόρας precede the word ἥκει? We cannot know *a priori* what kind of answer we shall get, if we ever get one; we must be prepared for an answer in any of the following categories:

(i) In phonological terms, e.g. 'the longer word precedes the shorter', or 'a word beginning with a consonant precedes a word beginning with a vowel'.[2]

(ii) In morphological terms, e.g. 'nouns precede verbs, irrespective of their syntactical interrelation'.

(iii) In syntactical terms, e.g. 'the subject precedes the predicate'.

(iv) In semantic terms, e.g. 'words denoting motion come at the end'.

(v) In lexical terms, e.g. 'ἥκει is one of *n* words which always come at the end'.

(vi) In logical terms, e.g. 'Hippocrates knows that Socrates will guess that someone has come, but he won't know who; so he utters

[1] This example is discussed by Goodell, pp. 30f., and Denniston, *Prose*, pp. 44f.

[2] Cf. Jacobsohn (ctr. Spitzer) and Wackernagel, *Wstregel.*

first the word which is least expected by his hearer'. Here and subsequently I use the word 'logical' in a highly general sense, as an adjective corresponding to the noun 'thought'.[1]

(vii) In emotive terms, e.g. 'the word Πρωταγόρας comes first because it is the focus of the speaker's emotion'.

(viii) In social or ceremonial terms, e.g. 'Protagoras is older than the speaker' or 'ἥκει is a tabu word in the speaker's family'.[2]

(ix) In terms involving the individual history of the speaker, e.g. 'the last time he said, or wrote, or thought "Protagoras has arrived" it was in the form Πρωταγόρας ἥκει, and the present example is determined by habit'.

(x) In stylistic or aesthetic terms, e.g. 'the last time he thought or said or wrote "Protagoras has arrived", it was in the form ἥκει Πρωταγόρας, and he likes variety of formulation'.

I should not like to think that these ten categories are an exhaustive list;[3] but they are something to go on with. The customary procedure in an enquiry of this kind is:

(i) To select one of these categories for exploration.

(ii) To formulate, within that category, hypothetical rules of the highest level of generality compatible with their being mutually exclusive.

(iii) To make a selection of texts which is random from the point of view of the rules to be tested but not necessarily random from the point of view of history, dialect or genre.

(iv) To compile statistics of the observance and non-observance of the rules.

(v) On the basis of these statistics, to distinguish between 'normal' and 'abnormal' order.

(vi) To discover the determinants of abnormality; that is to say, to discover conditions which are present in all the abnormal

[1] Goodell, pp. 14ff., uses 'rhetorical' in something like this sense.

[2] I exaggerate here, but cf. Wackernagel, *Wf.* pp. 47ff., for respects in which word order may reflect social conditions and changes in order changes in conditions.

[3] One must also consider e.g. 'mimetic' order, in which words denoting sudden noise or movement precede the words denoting its cause or source (Ammann, *Unt.* 1, p. 15, *Dopp.* p. 23; Havers, *Hdb.* p. 146), and 'excitant' order, in which the words which are essential to the hearer's understanding of the whole situation communicated are postponed in order to create tension (Lindhamer, p. 71; de Vries, pp. 87ff.).

instances but absent from all the normal, or, if present in some normal instances, are counteracted there by certain other conditions which are absent from the normal. The process of counteraction may, of course, be complex, so that we eventually find ourselves formulating rules which constitute exceptions to an exception to an exception to an exception to an exception to the general rule.

This procedure is not only customary,[1] but in some form or other inevitable. Yet the difficulties and dangers inherent in it are numerous and remarkable.

(i) Statistics may or may not give a clear picture; we cannot know until we have them. If, for example, we are testing the syntactical rule 'the subject precedes the predicate', and we find that the ratio of *SP* to *PS* is 10:1, we can embark with some confidence on the next stage of the enquiry, the discovery of the determinants of abnormality. On the other hand, if the ratio is 2:1 or lower, it is unlikely that we have discovered a primary determinant of order and more likely that we are on the track of a secondary phenomenon.

(ii) It is easy, but wrong, to equate 'statistically normal' with 'natural' and 'statistically abnormal' with 'distorted', 'inverted', etc. If, for example, we were investigating a language in which the order *SP* was invariable in statements and the order *PS* invariable in questions, it would be misleading to formulate the rule in terms such as: '*SP* is normal, but this normal order is reversed in questions'. Statements are more numerous than questions, but that is not a fact of a kind with which we are concerned; we should content ourselves with the pair of discoveries that (*a*) statement determines the order *SP*, (*b*) interrogation determines the order *PS*.

(iii) It is also easy, but equally wrong, to define the determinants of abnormality positively and to leave those of normal order negatively defined. Suppose, for example, that there is a language in which the order *PS* is statistically abnormal and in all instances of *PS* the predicate is the focus of the speaker's emotion. It is misleading, in such a case, to say that the predicate precedes when it is

[1] The distinction between 'habitual', 'traditional', 'usual', 'banal', or 'natural' order on the one hand and 'occasional' or 'rhetorical' order on the other is fundamental in Brugmann, *Vgl.* p. 677, Delbrück, *Vgl.* pp. 38, 110ff., *Altind.* p. 13, Schwyzer, *Gr.* II, p. 691, Leumann, p. 610, Kieckers, *St. Vbs.* pp. 2ff.; cf. Chantraine, pp. 71f., Vendryes, p. 168.

emotionally emphasised but omit to say that the subject also precedes when it is emotionally emphasised. It would be more useful to say that (*a*) the element which is the focus of emotion precedes, and (*b*) a syntactical determinant operates when emotion is absent. (Perhaps here, as in other aspects of linguistics, there is room for 'zero grade' as a positive concept.) We might also find in some language that normal and abnormal orders are equally positive manifestations of a single general principle.

(iv) No scholar, I suppose, thinks that he needs to be warned against regarding the order of his native language as 'natural', but the danger is more complex and more insidious than is commonly realised. The concepts 'nature' and 'instinct' die hard in linguistics. If in our browsing in linguistic literature we encounter an illustration of word order drawn from a North American Indian language, we think it fantastic; but because most of us who know Greek at all began to learn it as children, and became accustomed to it gradually, we fail to see that the fundamental differences in order between Plato's language and ours are at least as great as that between Sitting Bull's and ours.[1] One consequence of this failure is our tendency to regard as 'natural' such elements as are common to Greek and English order; we therefore seek explanations of the differences, but do not trouble to explain what is familiar; theses are written about καὶ ἀγλαὰ δέχθαι ἄποινα (*Il.* I, 23)[2] but not about φέρων τ' ἀπερείσι' ἄποινα (*ibid.* 13).[3] The fallacy is not wholly irrational in origin. Since Greek and English are the result of differentiation from much more obviously related originals, and since there exist language-families in which all the members of the family follow the same principles of word order, it might be supposed that we can find a Greek norm of order which will also be an Indo-European order and will be manifested also in English, French and German. We might find this; but we have no right whatsoever to *expect* that we shall find it. Indeed, when we reflect that the

[1] Cf. especially the phenomena discussed by Vahlen, p. 1002, Schöne, *Umstr.*, Wilhelm, *Synt.* Postgate, p. 166, appreciates the magnitude of the difference, but in describing it somewhat exaggerates the rational and intellectual aspects of Greek order.

[2] On 'Spaltung', 'Sperrung', and 'Hyperbaton' see Bachhammer, Havers, *Spalt.*, Lindhamer, de Vries, Rass, Kühner, II, pp. 600ff., Fraenkel, *Iktus*, pp. 162ff.

[3] Cf. the pertinent criticisms made by Loepfe, p. 10.

few thousand contemporary languages on which we have some information and the handful which we can trace back into the past represent only a tiny portion of the whole field of human language, and that within that portion the variety of structure which we can find is almost as great as the variety which we can imagine, we may well conclude that we have no right to expect anything.

Before we make our initial choice from the list of ten categories, let us remind ourselves of some important facts by a glance at the practice of modern spoken English. If we were asked by a foreigner for a general rule of word order in English, we should say, I suppose: The subject precedes the predicate. On second thoughts, we should add: That is, in a statement the subject must precede the predicate; any utterance in which part of the predicate, in the form of an auxiliary verb, precedes the subject is a question.

We shall have more than second thoughts, but let us consider for a moment the nature of our statement so far as it has gone. Our immediate classification of English sentences is in syntactical terms, according to whether the subject precedes the predicate or the predicate the subject. Yet the determinants of these alternative orders are not themselves syntactical; they are logical. Even then, the rule is not absolute; for there are questions which in respect of order are indistinguishable from statements, e.g., 'You haven't done it?', and the classification of the logical conditions which determine order in questions is subtle and difficult.[1]

Furthermore, our statement that the subject precedes the predicate in indicative statements is not entirely true. Consider, for example, 'Here comes a policeman', 'There goes a bus', 'Never have I heard such nonsense', or 'He would not do it, nor would I expect him to'. The importance of these exceptions lies in the fact that they are not instances of subordinate syntactical rules concerning negatives or demonstratives or adverbs or conjunctions; they are instances of the occurrence of specified words in specified patterns, and their usage can be communicated to a foreigner only by exhaustive lists and examples.

This reminds us that we cannot expect to find that the determinants of order in any language are all of one type. Determinants

[1] Cf. Brugmann, *Vschd.* pp. 1 ff.

of several different types may, as it were, pull a given utterance in different directions, and the order in which it is eventually formulated will represent the victory of one type of determinant over the others.[1]

The co-existence of determinants of different types is one of the fundamental facts of language. If I construct a sentence containing a subject and a verb which I have never used before—because, let us say, someone has just invented them—my unthinking grasp of a highly general and abstract syntactical rule will ensure that I put the subject before the verb. But this application of a rule to an unfamiliar content does not weaken my adherence to certain familiar patterns which are in conflict with the rule, such as 'nor would I expect him to'. Historically speaking, over a long enough period the balance of power between determinants demonstrably shifts;[2] but it would be a very unusual language in which all the utterances of a given individual speaker were wholly and exhaustively determined by mutually exclusive rules belonging all to the same type.

With these considerations in mind, let us turn back to our Greek example, Πρωταγόρας ἥκει, and make our first choice of a type of determinant for further exploration. It is clear that not all the ten types listed afford an equal purchase. The phonological type offers no firm purchase at all; rhythmically, the word Πρωταγόρας is choriambic; accentually, it is paroxytone with a short penultimate vowel; it begins with a consonant, and ends with one; its vowels are all back-vowels. The number of ways in which Πρωταγόρας can be seen to differ phonologically from ἥκει is very large, and the possible phonological reasons for the order Πρωταγόρας ἥκει are accordingly so numerous that no obvious starting-point of enquiry suggests itself. Similarly, if the determinant of the order is habit, or ceremonial, or aesthetic variation, it will not normally be discoverable. When the author is dead, there are limits to the inferences we can draw from what he has left us in writing.

The fact that some types of answer are hard to obtain does not mean that these answers are wrong; it means only that we shall be

[1] Schwyzer, *Gr.* II, p. 690. Firbas, *Comm.* pp. 39f., *WO*, p. 73 speaks of 'hierarchies of principles' and illustrates the growth of the domination of syntactical principles of order in English.

[2] Bloomfield, pp. 156f.

unwise to attempt such an answer until we have first explored the possibilities of easier types. The possibility of an answer in lexical or semantic terms depends in the first instance on observation and thereafter on statistical compilation or negative observation. The process reveals that there are many words in Greek which never begin a sentence, and others which never end one. In addition, there are some which are disproportionately common at the beginning of a sentence. These data are useful, but they do not help us with Πρωταγόρας ἥκει.

An answer in morphological or syntactical terms stands at the opposite extreme to the phonological. Morphological and syntactical categories in Greek are few, and the possible alternative rules of order in terms of these categories are correspondingly few. Also, there is seldom room for disagreement on whether a given word is noun or verb, subject or object or predicate.[1] The *a priori* advantage of a morphological or syntactical answer is strengthened by the fact that in very many languages the determinants of order are syntactical[2] and may be thought to be strengthened by ancient theory. The order subject–verb is described by Demetrius *Eloc.* 199 as 'natural' (ἡ φυσικὴ τάξις), and noun–verb by Dionysius *Comp. Verb.* 5 as τῇ φύσει ἑπόμενον. But any inclination which the statistician may feel to welcome the ancient critics as allies may falter when he considers their reasons. Demetrius, speaking specifically of narrative, says that the subject-matter (τὸ περὶ οὗ) of a sentence should be stated first, and ὅ τοῦτό ἐστιν second, which is not quite the same as saying that the syntactical subject precedes the syntactical predicate. He continues: 'but, of course, the order can be reversed.... I do not unconditionally approve the former order and condemn the latter; I am merely setting forth τὸ φυσικὸν εἶδος τῆς τάξεως.' Demetrius's conception of 'nature' is not necessarily based on linguistic usage, as we may see from Dionysius. Dionysius thinks it natural that nouns should precede verbs because nouns denote substance (οὐσία) whereas verbs denote accident (συμβεβηκός) and substance is 'by nature' prior to accident. He once believed, he says, that in order to write well we should follow nature and put nouns before verbs; but he realised later that this *a priori* philoso-

[1] The problem of Greek order in general has usually been discussed in syntactical terms, e.g. by Chantraine, Frisk, Kühner and Schwyzer.

[2] Barth, pp. 22ff.

phical view of the relation between substance and accident was irrelevant to good writing. He deserves credit for his observation, and gratitude for the honesty with which he reveals the divergence of interest between metaphysics and linguistics. When we come to examine syntactical statistics, we shall do so without philosophical allies.

(iii) MATERIAL

It is proposed in the next three chapters to identify types of determinant in Greek word order; it is therefore necessary to define 'Greek' for this limited purpose.

Clearly our enquiry must be into early Greek; the study of word order in the Gospels or Plutarch is interesting and worth-while, but no one will want to turn first to them for an answer to a question about the structure of the Greek language so long as the material of earlier centuries is available.[1] Equally clearly, our attention must be concentrated on prose rather than poetry. In poetry rhythm is among the determinants of form;[2] and where the determinants of form generally are more numerous, the isolation of the determinants of word order in particular is likely to be more difficult. This consideration is responsible also for my comparative neglect of that large portion of fourth-century prose in which rhythmical and phonetic preoccupations are demonstrably at work among the forces determining the form in which authors express themselves.

I have therefore paid special attention to Herodotus and documentary inscriptions. I am aware that Herodotus was an artist, the power and beauty of whose work are manifest on every page; yet there are two important respects in which his language is 'natural'. He does not try, as Thucydides constantly tries, to say too much in too few words; nor does he wrestle clumsily with language in the manner of the so-called 'Old Oligarch'. Secondly, the rhythmical and

[1] The statistics in Frisk, pp. 16ff., show important differences in syntactical order between Hellenistic and Classical Greek; we may perhaps come to the conclusion that the major difference is the emergence in Hellenistic Greek of syntactical determinants which are irrelevant to Classical Greek.

[2] Porzig, p. 97, says that the exigencies of metre do not create new patterns of order but only determine the author's choice between existing alternatives. I am not sure that this distinction does not beg the question; cf. Wackernagel, *Dicht.* pp. 6ff.; Bloomfield, pp. 157f., 165; Spiegel, p. 514.

phonetic considerations conspicuous in the fourth century are not in evidence in Herodotus.[1]

As for inscriptions, it must be admitted that Greek documentary inscriptions exhibit, at certain times and places, positive characteristics of their own, and that we cannot assume without qualification that their language is 'basic' or 'natural' Greek. Nevertheless, these characteristics are few and easily identifiable; the establishment of formulae, even at Athens, was remarkably late; and there are several other considerations which make inscriptions of prime importance to the student of word order. First, the manuscripts and papyri of a prose literary text reveal just enough differences in respect of order to make us reluctant to rely too heavily on the authenticity of the order in any one passage, whereas an inscription may be presumed to be only one stage removed from an autograph, and slips of the chisel are likely to be rarer than slips of the pen.[2] Secondly, the composition of documentary inscriptions is motivated by a desire to communicate clearly and not to invite admiration as a work of art.[3] I have therefore chosen several of my documentary examples from places which were not centres of cultural and literary development. I cannot swear that the decrees of the Ozolian Locrians do not betray the hand of a mute inglorious Gorgias, but I may be allowed to doubt that and to believe that in early documents from the Peloponnese, the North-West and Crete the influence of *Kunstprosa* is minimal. There is some value in applying to word order, and to all problems in the history of the Greek language, a principle which was applied on a famous occasion to a matter of higher importance: πρῶτον ἐν ταῖς πόλεσι ȝητήσωμεν ποῖόν τί ἐστιν.

[1] Herodotus's language undeniably shows some characteristics which we associate with spoken rather than with written composition (cf. Pohlenz, *Herodot* (Leipzig, 1937), pp. 209f.), and this makes analysis of the logical relations between the elements of a Herodotean utterance easier and more profitable (cf. Loepfe, p. 59).

[2] Striking and characteristic patterns of order in literature are always in danger of over-systematic emendation, from which inscriptions are comparatively safe (Schöne, *Umstr.* pp. 145ff.).

[3] Schick, pp. 362f.

CHAPTER II

LEXICAL AND SEMANTIC DETERMINANTS

(i) POSTPOSITIVES AND PREPOSITIVES

Most Greek words are 'mobile' (symbol *M*), in the sense that any one of them may be found at the beginning of a clause, at its end, or in the middle. There are, however, two important categories of limited mobility. These are:

(I) *Postpositives* (symbol *q*). These words never, or only in certain specifiable circumstances, occur at the beginning of a clause. Some of them are unconditionally *q*, i.e. may not in any circumstances begin a clause. They are:

(i) The particles ἄρα (ῥα), αὖ, γάρ, γε, δαί, δέ, δῆτα, θην, μέν, μήν (μάν), οὖν (ὦν), περ, τε.

(ii) The word τοι, which may be regarded either as a pronoun or as a particle, according to dialect.

(iii) The pronouns με, μου (μευ), μοι, μιν (νιν), σφε.

(iv) The modal particle ἄν and its synonyms κε and κα.

Certain others may conveniently be treated as unconditionally *q*, since the circumstances in which they may begin a clause are extremely restricted and the instances very few:

(v) δή.

(vi) The pronouns οἱ and σφι.

(vii) The oblique cases of αὐτός in the anaphoric sense. In the sense 'self' they are *M*; but although this semantic difference might be expected to cause trouble, I know of no instance of initial αὐτ-όν, etc. which requires to be translated as anaphoric and forbids the translation 'self'.

The status of other *q* is less sharply defined:

(viii) The rule that the indefinite pronouns, adjectives and adverbs τις, πως, etc. are *q* is true on the whole, but to some extent artificially protected by conventions of accent and translation. Presented with τις ἔνδον; as a complete utterance, we should write an acute accent on τίς and translate 'who is in?' even when 'is someone in?' might seem more appropriate to the context.[1]

[1] Is A. *Ag.* 1344 σῖγα· τίς πληγὴν ἀϋτεῖ καιρίως οὐτασμένος; really a question?

(ix) The pronouns σε, σου, σοι, when initial, are by convention accented and are translated as emphatic. When medial or final, they are written as enclitic if the context permits their translation as unemphatic but accented if it requires them to be translated as emphatic. The statement 'unemphatic σε, σου, σοι are enclitic and postpositive' thus incurs the danger of circularity inherent in the concept 'emphasis'.

(x) Similar difficulties beset the classification of νῦν/νῦν, the oblique cases of σφεῖς, the present tense of φάναι, and the oblique cases of ἡμεῖς and ὑμεῖς, though the two last lack the complication of accentual conventions.

(xi) The verb εἶναι cannot be classed as *q* without many qualifications and reservations, not all of which admit of a satisfactory classification. εἶναι as copula tends, in most authors, to be treated as *q*; when it is first word in a clause, we import into its translation nuances which the context does not always demand and sometimes scarcely justifies. I use the symbol M^q for εἶναι in its copulative sense.

In generalising about *q* it is the unconditional *q*, categories (i)–(vii), which I have in mind, and it is the use of these words especially which my examples are designed to illustrate.

The definition of *q* as words which never begin a clause necessitates a modification of our definition of 'clause'. One such modification is discussed below. The other is that vocatives, oaths and parentheses, although often marked off by commas in modern texts, are often immediately followed by *q*, e.g. Ar. *Pax* 137 ἀλλ' ὦ μέλ' ἄν μοι σιτίων διπλῶν ἔδει; Pl. *Prm.* 137B τίς οὖν, εἰπεῖν, μοι ἀποκρινεῖται; This amounts to saying that in respect of *q* vocatives, etc. do not affect the order.[1]

(II) *Prepositives* (symbol *p*).[2] These words never, or only in certain specifiable circumstances, end a clause. They are:

(i) ἀλλά, ἀτάρ (αὐτάρ), ἤ, ἦ, καί, οὐδέ (μηδέ), οὔτε (μήτε), εἴτε.

(ii) μή='lest'.

(iii) Relatives, including the indeclinables εἰ, ἐπεί, ἵνα, etc.

(iv) ὁ='the'. In other senses ὁ is not *p*.

[1] Wackernagel, *Gesetz*, pp. 391f.; Kieckers, *Vb. Sag.* p. 150. The most remarkable postponement of *q* is in a *v.l.* at Ar. *Nu.* 398f. καὶ πῶς, ὦ μῶρε σὺ καὶ Κρονίων ὄζων καὶ βεκκεσέληνε, εἴπερ βάλλει τοὺς ἐπιόρκους, δῆτ' οὐχὶ Σίμων' ἐνέπρησεν; (δῆτ' V: πῶς codd. plerique: πῶς δῆτ' contra metrum R al.). See also p. 15 n. 1, p. 16 n. 3.

[2] Ammann, *Unt.* 1, p. 12.

(v) Prepositions. In this category considerable historical changes and differences between genres are observable, but in prose generally all the prepositions are *p* except sometimes περί; ἄνευ, ἕνεκα, χάριν, χωρίς, etc., reasonably classified as 'improper' prepositions, do not come under consideration here.

The simple negative is not easy to classify. It has obvious *p* characteristics; it might be argued that expressions such as εἰ δὲ μή or ὧδε μὲν ἂν γένοιτο, ἐκείνως δ' οὔ are just as elliptic as e.g. οὐκ οἶδ' ὅπου, and therefore do not tell against its inclusion among *p*. Since, however, it may constitute a complete utterance by itself, and since the types of clause in which it may appear last are numerous, I do not treat it as *p*.

The three types of minimal complete utterance are $\|M\|$, $\|pM\|$ and $\|Mq\|$. By definition, $\|p\|$, $\|q\|$, $\|Mp\|$ and $\|qM\|$ are impossible. When two M and one q constitute a complete utterance, the two arrangements which are theoretically possible are $\|Mq\ M\|$ and $\|M\ Mq\|$; with two M and two q, there are three possible orders, $\|Mqq\ M\|$, $\|Mq\ Mq\|$ and $\|M\ Mqq\|$; with three M and two q, six possible orders; and so on. Yet these alternatives are not equally used. Greek has a strongly marked preference for $\|Mq(q\ldots)\ M\ (M\ldots)$, accumulating q after the first M.[1] This is an observable historical fact which could never have been deduced from the definitions of M, p and q. In this pattern word-groups which we, as speakers of modern European languages, would regard as indissoluble are disrupted, e.g. Callinus, fr. I, 20 ὥσπερ γάρ μιν πύργον ἐν ὀφθαλμοῖσιν ὁρῶσιν, Ar. *Nu.* 257 ὥσπερ με τὸν 'Αθάμανθ' ὅπως μὴ θύσετε, *DGE*, 412, 3 (Olympia, VI B.C.) ἁ δέ κα ϝράτρα ἁ δαμοσία τελεία εἴη δικάδδōσα, Hdt. VI, 63, 2 ἐν δέ οἱ ἐλάσσονι χρόνῳ... ἡ γυνὴ αὕτη τίκτει. Similarly, words which, as we should say, 'go together in sense' are widely separated,[2] e.g. Lys. I, 17 ταῦτά μου πάντα εἰς τὴν γνώμην εἰσῄει; in particular, q which 'belong' in participial and infinitive clauses are commonly associated with the words to which those clauses are subordinate, e.g. Hom. *Il.* XXI, 347 χαίρει δέ μιν ὅστις ἐθείρῃ (a rare type), Hdt. I, 30, 4 καί σφι εἶδε ἅπασι τέκνα ἐκγενόμενα, D. l, 18 ἐκέλευσά μοι αὐτὸν ναύτας μισθώσασθαι. Hence a sentence such as Pl. *Euthyphro* 6A φήσει τίς με

[1] Wackernagel, *Gesetz*; Schwyzer, *Gr.* II, p. 692; Leumann, pp. 611 ff.; Delbrück, *Altind.* pp. 47 f., 59.

[2] Cf. Brugmann, *Vgl.* pp. 681 ff.; Delbrück, *Vgl.* pp. 40 ff.

ἐξαμαρτάνειν is to be treated as only an apparent example, not a real example, of a *q* (με) beginning a clause.[1]

Generally speaking, the earlier the Greek, the more closely does $M+M+q>Mq\,M$ approximate to a rule. It is not, however, a question of certain metrically convenient patterns establishing themselves in the dactylic hexameter and influencing the subsequent development of the language. The phenomenon occurs in other Indo-European languages, especially in Indo-Iranian, e.g. Old Persian, XPa (Xerxes, Persepolis) 15 *uta-maiy tya pitā akunauš* = καί μου ὅτι (ὁ) πατὴρ ἐποίησεν.[2]

The progressive tendency in post-Homeric Greek to distribute *q* within the clause, instead of concentrating them after the leading *M*, is a secondary phenomenon. One of its principal causes is a certain development, independent of anything we have discussed so far, in the treatment of *p*. Even in the earliest Greek there exists a tendency to arrange an utterance consisting of *M*, *p* and *q* in the order *pMq*, and this tendency is increasingly strengthened in historical times. This, again, is an observable fact which could not have been deduced from definitions. Its extreme development may be seen in the evolution of 'compound verbs'. By the end of the fifth century prefix and verb were virtually indissoluble in the language of prose, and were presumably already an accentual unit. This evolution may be symbolised $M_1q+M_2>M_3q$. Contemporaneously with the coalescence of *p* and *M*, certain words underwent semantic changes and declined from *M*-status to *p*-status. The demonstrative pronoun ὁ in Homeric Greek may be symbolised M^p, i.e. *M* destined to become *p* (and, of course, already in process of change even in Homer).

The coalescence of *p* and *M* is most clearly seen in cases of *pMq* where *q* is a connecting particle, e.g. Hom. *Il.* XXIV, 665 τῇ δεκάτῃ δέ κε θάπτοιμεν, Hdt. IX, 49, 3 ἀπὸ τοῦ ποταμοῦ γάρ σφι οὐκ ἐξῆν ὕδωρ φορέεσθαι, Ar. *Nu.* 1198 ὅπερ οἱ προτένθαι γὰρ δοκοῦσί μοι παθεῖν. These three examples may be symbolised: Hom., *pMqq M*;

[1] The MS. text of E. *IA* 1435 παῦσαί με μὴ κάκιζε, accepted by Wackernagel, *Gesetz*, p. 392, might be tolerable if the context permitted (as it does not) the translation 'stop abusing me'. Occasionally the inversion of *M* and *q* normal in sentences of the type φησί με ἐξαμαρτάνειν is found where some degree of pause immediately before *q* seems inescapable, e.g. Lys. XII, 10 ὤμοσεν...λαβὼν τὸ τάλαντόν με σώσειν. Cf. p. 13 n. 1 and p. 16 n. 3.

[2] Kent, pp. 96f.; Wackernagel, *Gesetz*, p. 404.

Hdt., $ppMqq\ M\ M\ M\ M$; Ar., $ppMq\ Mq\ M$. More commonly, the pM complex may be disrupted by connecting particles, but not by other q, e.g. Pl. *Prt.* 310 C ὁ γάρ τοι παῖς με ὁ Σάτυρος ἀπέδρα, where the pattern is $pqqMq\ pM\ M$. This pattern is typical.

The placing of particles after the definite article or preposition is so fundamental a characteristic of Greek, and we learn it so early in our study of the language, that we do not reflect often enough how curious a phenomenon it is. It is in fact the result of a compromise between pattern and principle. On the one hand, there is the increasing tendency to treat pM as an indissoluble unit; on the other hand, there is a poetic language in which $pq(q\ldots)\ M$ is unrestricted and the evolution $M^p > p$ only in its initial stages. Symbolically, pq_1Mq_2, where q_1 is a connecting particle and q_2 any other q, is the joint product of $pq(q\ldots)\ M$, $M^pq(q\ldots)\ M$, and $pMq(q\ldots)$.[1]

As we should expect, the treatment of $p+M+q$ varies greatly from one dialect to another and from one period to another. Herodotus, for example, inserts a q pronoun between article and noun or between preposition and noun; in Attic prose this is very rare with μοι, even rarer with σοι, and unexampled with those cases of αὐτόν which are equivalent to μιν, οἱ, σφι. καί μοι and ἀλλά μοι with imperatives survive more strongly in Attic than any other καὶ qM or ἀλλὰ qM where q is a pronoun. A literal translation of *DGE*, 412, 3 into Attic—τὸ δ' ἂν ψήφισμα τὸ δημόσιον κύριον εἴη δικάζον—although not entirely unparalleled,[2] would be extremely unusual. Thucydides commonly places anaphoric αὐτ- immediately after connective καί; this is not favoured by fourth-century prose. On the other hand, fourth-century writers arrange the words in certain parentheses to yield $M(q)\,(|)\,qM\ldots$ in preference to $M(q)|\,Mq\ldots$, e.g. D. 1, 19 'τί οὖν;' ἄν τις εἴποι, 'σὺ γράφεις ταῦτ' εἶναι στρατιωτικά;', Pl. *Euthd.* 297 C νεωστί, μοι δοκεῖν, καταπεπλευκότι.[3] The deferment of connecting particles also provides evidence of the formation of other types of complex unit. One common type consists of a word repeated in polyptosis, or a pair of closely related

[1] Cf. Leo, p. 419.

[2] E.g. Th. VI, 64, 1 τοὺς γὰρ ἂν ψιλοὺς...τοὺς ἱππέας...βλάπτειν ἂν μεγάλα. For other types of pqM which are unevenly distributed among dialects cf. Wackernagel, *Anr.* pp. 27 ff. (on ἐάν τις and αἴ τίς κα) and Wilhelm, *Beitr.* pp. 44 f. (on τῶν τις πολιτῶν).

[3] Wackernagel, *Gesetz*, pp. 392, 397. Cf. p. 13 n. 1, p. 15 n. 1.

words, e.g. A. *Eu.* 529 ἄλλ' ἄλλᾳ δ' ἐφορεύει. This accords with such phenomena as παρὰ φίλος φίλῳ and ὑπὲρ αὐτὸς αὑτοῦ.[1] A numeral and the word to which it refers are sometimes treated as indissoluble,[2] e.g. *SEG*, x, 2 (Marathon, VI/V B.C.), 19ff. τριάκοντα ἄνδρ[ας δὲ] τὸν ἀγο͂να ἐπιόφσασθαι.

Complex units account for many clauses in which *q* are not placed immediately after the leading *M*, but there is another phenomenon of much wider significance. Contrast Hdt. I, 10, 2 καὶ ἡ γυνὴ ἐπορᾷ μιν ἐξιόντα with 12, 1 καί μιν ἐκείνη ἐγχειρίδιον δοῦσα κατακρύπτει. In 12, 1 the pattern *pqM*... is normal; in 10, 2 we have *ppM Mq M*. Now the idea that καὶ ἡ γυνὴ ἐπορᾷ constitute a complex unit cannot be taken seriously; and the fact that in reading the narrative slowly and clearly we would make a slight pause between γυνή and ἐπορᾷ is highly relevant. The example suggests that *q* are not necessarily placed after the leading *p* or *M* of what would traditionally be defined as a 'clause', but may occupy a similar position within one of the word-groups which constitute the clause; a 'word-group' being recognisable by the pauses of the voice which precede and follow it.[3] This suggestion is supported by very many passages, e.g. Th. VI, 9, 3 καὶ πρὸς μὲν τοὺς τρόπους τοὺς ὑμετέρους ἀσθενὴς ἄν μου ὁ λόγος εἴη. The words καὶ... ὑμετέρους are not a 'clause', but they are a well-defined word-group; ἀσθενής begins the next group, which takes the familiar form *Mqq pM M^q*.

A word-group, defined in terms of natural pause, may be very short,[4] as in Hdt. I, 2, 1 ταῦτα μὲν δὴ ἴσα πρὸς ἴσα σφι γενέσθαι (note that ἴσα πρὸς ἴσα are treated, as we should expect, as a complex unit), Lys. II, 2 ὅμως δὲ ὁ μὲν λόγος μοι περὶ τούτων, ὁ δ' ἀγών κτλ. Indeed, circumstances often arise in which we may wonder whether the first word of a clause is to be followed by a slight pause or is simply equivalent to *p*, e.g. Pl. *Prt.* 333B οὐκοῦν ἓν ἂν εἴη ἡ σωφροσύνη καὶ ἡ σοφία.

One effect of breaking up a clause into word-groups is to distribute *q*; and one consequence of this distribution is that *q* are often to

[1] Cf. Haupt, pp. 184ff.; Schulze mentions the phenomenon in Lithuanian.

[2] Cf. Fraenkel, *Iktus*, pp. 120ff.

[3] Fraenkel, *Kolon*, pp. 319ff.; de Vries, pp. 20f. See also p. 19 n. 1.

[4] 'Kurzkola' in Fraenkel, *Kolon*, pp. 327, 343, *al.* Section (iii) below is relevant.

be found in close proximity to the words with which, as we should say, they 'go'.[1] As speakers of modern English, we find Pl. *Euthyphro* 9 C τούτου μὲν ἀφίημί σε and 15 E νῦν γὰρ σπεύδω ποι more 'natural' than τούτου μέν σ' ἀφίημι and νῦν γάρ ποι σπεύδω. We are therefore bound to consider the possibility that the fundamental reason for the distribution of *q* and the consequent departure from the original tendency to collect *q* after the leading *M* of the clause is not the fact that a clause can often be broken up into word-groups but a desire to bring closer together words which 'go together' in sense. We might suspect that we see the result of a conflict between pattern and sense in those clauses in which *q* is repeated, e.g. E. *Md.* 250f. ὡς τρὶς ἂν παρ' ἀσπίδα στῆναι θέλοιμ' ἂν μᾶλλον ἢ τεκεῖν ἅπαξ (*pMq pM M Mq M pM M*). ἄν is the *q* most commonly repeated,[2] but others may be,[3] e.g. X. *Cyr.* IV, 5, 29 σκέψαι δὲ οἴῳ ὄντι μοι περὶ σὲ οἷος ὢν περὶ ἐμὲ ἔπειτά μοι μέμφῃ ($Mq \,|||\, M\ M^q q\ pM \,|||\, M\ M^q\ pM \,|||\, Mq\ M$). This phenomenon is not confined to Greek, but occurs also in Vedic Sanskrit, e.g. *Ṛgveda* I, 35, 11 *tebhir no adya pathibhiḥ sugebhī rakṣā ca no adhi ca brūhi* = ταύταις ἡμᾶς τήμερον ὁδοῖς εὐβάτοις σῷζέ τε ἡμᾶς ὑπέρ τε (ἡμῶν) ἀγόρευε, where the pronoun *no* (<*naḥ*) is placed both after the leading word (*tebhiḥ*) of the whole clause and, with the postpositive *ca*, after the leading word (*rakṣā*) of the second half of the clause; it happens also to be the object of *rakṣā*.[4]

I doubt, however, whether the distribution of *q* over the constituent word-groups of a clause is motivated to any significant degree by the desire to bring together words which 'belong together'. There are a limited number of associations with ἄν: οὐκ ἄν, ἴσως ἄν, τάχ' ἄν, ἡδέως ἄν, etc.;[5] but the many clauses in which distribution

[1] Compare the history of Russian -ся (Delbrück, *Vgl.* p. 50); Macdonell, p. 285.

[2] Kühner, I, pp. 246ff.

[3] Kühner, I, p. 660, where, however, sentences of entirely different types are treated without discrimination.

[4] Dr A. K. Warder provides me with a remarkable example of repeated *q* from an early Sanskrit drama: *yā te ruṣṭā, sā te nāhaṃ* = ἥτις σοι ὀργισθεῖσα, αὕτη σοι οὐκ ἐγώ, where the second *te* is meaningful only in the light of the first.

[5] These associations are specially clear in the examples assembled by Fraenkel, *Kolon*, pp. 319ff. In D. IX, 70 πάλαι τις ἡδέως ἂν ἴσως ἐρωτήσων κάθηται the stereotyped association ἡδέως ἄν is responsible for the illusory appearance of 'ἄν with the future'.

has the effect which seems 'natural' to speakers of modern English are matched by an equally large number in which it has the opposite effect, e.g. [X.] *Resp. Ath.* 3, 10 δοκοῦσι δὲ Ἀθηναῖοι καὶ τοῦτό μοι οὐκ ὀρθῶς βουλεύεσθαι, D. XXI, 26 οὑναντίος ἧκεν ἂν εὐθύς μοι λόγος, Hdt. II, 17, 5 ἔστι δὲ καὶ ἕτερα διφάσια στόματα...τοῖσι οὐνόματα κεῖται τάδε, τῷ μὲν Σαϊτικὸν αὐτῶν, τῷ δὲ Μενδήσιον, [Lys.] XX, 9 τοὺς μὲν γὰρ ἐξήλαυνον αὐτῶν, τοὺς δ' ἀπεκτίννυσαν (ctr. And. I, 34 οἱ μὲν αὐτῶν φεύγοντες ᾤχοντο, οἱ δὲ συλληφθέντες ἀπέθανον), *SEG*, XII, 87 (336 B.C.), 21 f. καὶ ἡ οὐσία δημοσία ἔστω αὐτοῦ (ctr. *IG* II², 43 (377 B.C.), 55 f. καὶ τὰ χρήματα αὐτοῦ δημόσια ἔστω and III (362 B.C.), 41 f. καὶ τὴν οὐσίαν αὐτῶν δημοσίαν εἶναι). Hdt. I, 30, 2 νῦν ὦν ἵμερος ἐπειρέσθαι μοι ἐπῆλθέ σε εἴ τινα ἤδη εἶδες ὀλβιώτατον is a remarkable distribution. Occasionally, distribution may result even in a connecting particle being placed in the second word-group of the clause, e.g. Ar. *Ra.* 1434 ὁ μὲν σοφῶς γὰρ εἶπεν, ὁ δ' ἕτερος σαφῶς.

(ii) TYPES OF CLAUSE

In section (iii) I offer statistical data on the position of certain *M* within the clause, and in chapter III data on the relative positions of subject, verb and object. I have selected three texts for statistical analysis: Herodotus III, 61–87, Lysias XII (*In Eratosthenem*) and Plato, *Laches*.

Statistical data cannot be presented in terms of 'word-groups', for the analysis of a clause into word-groups is to some extent subjective and renders independent checking of the statistics impossible. With one exception, therefore (see (vi) below), I present the statistics in terms of 'clauses', with the reflection that if out of n_1 occurrences of a given word n_2 are at the beginning of a clause the fraction n_2/n_1 cannot be decreased by substituting 'word-group' for 'clause' and is almost certain to be increased.[1] In general, I follow the traditional

[1] If we divided into groups (as indicated by the dotted uprights) sentences such as Lys. XII, 24 ἐπὶ μὲν τῇ τούτου ὠφελείᾳ ⁝ καὶ πρὸς ἕτερον περὶ τούτου διαλέγεσθαι ⁝ ἀσεβὲς εἶναι νομίζω | ἐπὶ δὲ τῇ τούτου βλάβῃ ⁝ καὶ πρὸς αὐτὸν τοῦτον ⁝ ὅσιον καὶ εὐσεβές the conclusion which my statistics suggest would be greatly strengthened. This must not be taken to mean that the word-group as a unit can be disregarded in all statistical enquiry concerning word order. Its disregard is one of the main defects of discussion of syntactical order in terms of 'Mittelstellung' of the verb, as in Kieckers, *St. Vbs.* pp. 13 ff.

classification of clauses into 'main' (*mn.*),[1] 'subordinate' (*sb.*), 'participial' (*pt.*), and 'infinitive' (*inf.*), with the following modifications:

(i) When a *sb.* is divided into two or more members, of which all but the first are co-ordinated with what precedes by a connecting particle, I treat all but the first member as *mn.*

(ii) When one and the same noun or pronoun is both subject of a participle and subject or object of another verb, I associate it with the participle;[2] thus in Hdt. III, 61, 1 Καμβύσῃ δὲ τῷ Κύρου χρονίζοντι περὶ Αἴγυπτον...ἐπανιστέαται ἄνδρες μάγοι δύο I treat Καμβύσῃ...Αἴγυπτον as a type of *pt.* (*pt.**), Καμβύσῃ being the subject of χρονίζοντι, and in Lys. XII, 73 ἀναστὰς δὲ Θηραμένης ἐκέλευσεν ὑμᾶς, κτλ. I treat ἀναστὰς δὲ Θηραμένης as *pt.**

(iii) When a noun or pronoun is subject both of δοκεῖν, λέγεσθαι or φαίνεσθαι and of an infinitive or participle, I treat it as subject of the infinitive or participle. Thus I analyse ἀνὴρ δοκεῖ ἀδικεῖν as a type of *inf.* (*inf.**) ἀνὴρ...ἀδικεῖν and a *mn.* δοκεῖ.

(iv) Other types of complex are dismembered; thus I analyse Pl. *La.* 195 A πρὸς τί τοῦτ' εἶπες βλέψας; as (1) *mn.*, τοῦτ' εἶπες, (2) *pt.*, πρὸς τί...βλέψας.

(v) I include in my data participial and infinitive complexes with the definite article (*a/pt.* and *a/inf.*).

(vi) For the purpose of the next section, I give the status of 'clauses' to all word-groups introduced by a connecting particle, e.g. καὶ τὰ τοιαῦθ' ἅπαντα; these naturally do not enter into data on the interrelation of subject, verb and object.

(vii) I ignore throughout the existence of vocatives and oaths.

(iii) PREFERENTIAL WORDS

Certain *M* are disproportionately common at the beginning of a clause—or more precisely, as near the beginning as *p* will allow them to get. I call these words 'preferential' (symbol M^a); the most obvious categories are:

(i) Interrogatives.

(ii) Negatives.

[1] The category 'Nachsätze', i.e. *mn.* preceded by *sb.*, is sometimes treated separately, e.g. by Kieckers, *St. Vbs.* See p. 30 n. 1.

[2] Cf. Kieckers, *St. Vbs.* pp. 129ff.

(iii) The demonstrative pronoun ὁ.

(iv) Words which relate successive clauses as a whole one to another, e.g. πρῶτον, ἔπειτα, εἶτα, ὅμως.

In addition, the following categories must be considered:

(v) ἐγώ, ἐμέ, ἐμοῦ, ἐμοί (ἔγωγε, etc.).

(vi) σύ, ἡμεῖς, ὑμεῖς, in the nominative case; I leave out of account the oblique cases, for reasons given in II (i).

(vii) οὗτος, τοσοῦτος, τοιοῦτος, τηλικοῦτος (οὑτοσί, etc.).

(viii) οὕτω(ς) (οὑτωσί).

(ix) ἐκεῖνος.

(x) δεῦρο, ἐνταῦθα, ἐνταυθοῖ, ἐντεῦθεν.

(xi) ἐκεῖ, ἐκεῖσε, ἐκεῖθεν.

(xii) νῦν (νυνί, νυνδή).

(xiii) τότε.

(xiv) αὐτός='self'.

(xv) ὁ αὐτός.

(xvi) ἄλλος.

(xvii) ἕτερος.

(xviii) ἀμφότεροι.

(xix) πολύς, πλείων, πλεῖστος.

(xx) πολλάκις.

(xxi) εἷς.

I do not doubt that further enquiry would substantially enlarge the list of M^a; I have selected only the most obvious; but in this book I confine the term 'preferential' and the symbol M^a to the twenty-one categories listed above, together with two further categories specified below. All other M I call 'ordinary' (symbol M^b).

I give now statistical data of M^a in the three texts analysed. Column I lists the occurrences of the word concerned as the leading M of a clause which contains also at least one M^b; column II, its occurrences where it is preceded only by M^a and followed by at least one M^b; column III, where it is the only M of the clause or is preceded only by M^a and is not followed by any M^b; column IV, where its classification is doubtful, depending on one's classification of εἶναι, copulative γίγνεσθαι, or the oblique cases of σύ, ἡμεῖς, ὑμεῖς, σφεῖς; column V, where it is preceded by at least one M^b, whether or not it is also preceded by M^a. Thus from Hdt. III, 65, 1 τότε μὲν τοσαῦτα, τότε is put in column I, τοσαῦτα in column III;

in Lys. XII, 51 ὡς ἀμφότερα ταῦτα ἐγὼ πολλοῖς τεκμηρίοις παραστήσω, I classify ἀμφότερα in column I, ταῦτα, ἐγώ, πολλοῖς in column II.

			I	II	III	IV	V
(v)	ἐγώ, etc.	Hdt.	14	1	1	—	5
		Lys.	10	3	1	—	4
		Pl.	60	11	11	5	23
(vi)	σύ, etc.	Hdt.	6	—	—	—	1
		Lys.	16	1	—	—	—
		Pl.	33	8	3	1	13
(vii)	οὗτος, etc.	Hdt.	45	12	1	3	70
		Lys.	79	14	2	3	25
		Pl.	75	28	8	12	95
(viii)	οὕτως	Hdt.	5	1	—	—	2
		Lys.	9	—	—	—	1
		Pl.	11	6	1	—	8
(ix)	ἐκεῖνος	Hdt.	5	2	—	—	1
		Lys.	18	4	2	—	10
		Pl.	7	—	2	—	9
(x)	δεῦρο, etc.	Hdt.	5	—	—	—	1
		Lys.	1	1	—	—	1
		Pl.	—	1	—	—	4
(xi)	ἐκεῖ	Pl.	1	—	—	—	1
(xii)	νῦν	Hdt.	6	—	—	—	1
		Lys.	8	3	—	—	1
		Pl.	18	5	—	—	4
(xiii)	τότε	Hdt.	3	1	—	—	2
		Lys.	3	1	—	—	1
(xiv)	αὐτός	Hdt.	15	6	—	—	4
		Lys.	15	2	—	8	5
		Pl.	21	3	—	4	26
(xv)	ὁ αὐτός	Hdt.	3	1	—	—	1
		Lys.	4	2	—	1	3
		Pl.	4	1	1	2	3
(xvi)	ἄλλος	Hdt.	6	4	3	—	3
		Lys.	8	2	—	1	2
		Pl.	32	13	7	2	13

		I	II	III	IV	V
(xvii) ἕτερος	Hdt.	3	—	—	—	1
	Lys.	4	2	2	1	5
	Pl.	—	1	1	—	1
(xviii) ἀμφότεροι	Hdt.	2	—	—	—	2
	Lys.	4	—	—	—	—
	Pl.	—	—	1	—	—
(xix) πολύς, etc.	Hdt.	6	—	—	—	4
	Lys.	26	7	2	1	8
	Pl.	7	4	3	—	11
(xx) πολλάκις	Hdt.	1	—	—	—	—
	Lys.	2	—	—	—	—
	Pl.	3	—	—	—	1
(xxi) εἷς	Hdt.	3	—	—	—	3
	Lys.	1	3	—	—	—
	Pl.	3	3	—	2	1

It will be seen that there are differences between authors; the οὗτος group is overwhelmingly M^a in Lysias, much less so in Herodotus and Plato. Greater differences are apparent in:

(xxii) ὅδε, τῇδε, ὧδε, τοιόσδε, τοσόσδε.

(xxiii) πᾶς and adverbs formed with the stem παντ-.

		I	II	III	IV	V
(xxii) ὅδε, etc.	Hdt.	3	—	1	2	17
	Lys.	3	—	—	—	1
	Pl.	11	2	2	2	23
(xxiii) πᾶς	Hdt.	7	2	—	2	23
	Lys.	13	4	—	—	4
	Pl.	20	4	4	—	10
πάντως	Hdt.	2	—	—	—	—
	Lys.	1	—	—	—	—
	Pl.	4	—	1	—	1

Of the instances of ὅδε, etc. in column V, 16 out of 17 in Herodotus and 11 out of 23 in Plato actually occur as the *last* word of a clause.

Semantically, M^a do not constitute a well-defined class. One group has a purely demonstrative character,[1] e.g. ἐκεῖνος, and a second group consists of logical connectives,[2] e.g. ὅμως. Others have affinities with one or other of those two groups, as ἐγώ, σύ, etc. have with the demonstratives or πάντως with the logical connectives. Others have affinities with both, e.g. οὕτως and νῦν;[3] and others again with neither, e.g. πολύς.[4]

[1] Kieckers, *St. Vbs.* pp. 18ff., 110ff., 126f.; *Or. R.* I, p. 9; Kaibel, pp. 99f.; Bergaigne, p. 176. For statistics of pronominal M^a in relative *sb.*, in terms of *S* and *P*, see Frisk, p. 39.

[2] Bloch, *passim*.

[3] Ammann, *Unt.* I, p. 42.

[4] Ammann, *Unt.* I, p. 16. I have not exhausted the list of M^a; see Spiegel, p. 514, Kieckers, *Vb. Sag.* pp. 145ff., *Or. R.* I, p. 9, Schöne, *Vschr.* on 'say', and Bloch, pp. 243ff., Kieckers, *St. Vbs.* pp. 50ff., on 'be'. See also ch. IV, B (iv) below.

CHAPTER III

SYNTACTICAL DETERMINANTS

(i) GENERAL PRINCIPLES

In Greek prose of the fifth and fourth centuries B.C. the subject (*S*) tends to precede its verb (*V*); the relevant statistics can be broken down to show, for example, that in main clauses in Xenophon, *HG* the ratio *SV*: *VS* is 4·0, in relative clauses in Lysias 9·0, in temporal clauses in Herodotus 1·2, and so on. The ratio *OV*: *VO* shows greater fluctuation, the extremes being 0·7 and 4·0, but in most types of clause in most authors it exceeds 1·0.[1]

These ratios seem to justify us *prima facie* in giving *SV* and *OV* the status of syntactical rules. The problem is then to account for the instances of *VS* and *VO*, and this problem we might expect to solve by finding conditions which are present in all instances of *VS* or *VO* but absent from those of *SV* and *OV*, or, if present in *SV* and *OV*, are counteracted by other conditions absent from *VS* and *VO*... and so on.[2] If we confined ourselves to purely linguistic conditions, we might imagine that the differences of order between Lys. XIX, 50 ἠκούετε...ὡς Διότιμος ἔχοι τάλαντα τετταράκοντα πλείω ἢ ὅσα αὐτὸς ὡμολόγει and 51 ἁπάντων ἀκηκοότων ὅτι τετταράκοντα τάλαντα ἔχοι Διότιμος or between Pl. *Ion* 538B τί δὲ δὴ ὅταν Ὅμηρος λέγῃ ὡς...Ἑκαμήδη...δίδωσι and 538C τί δὲ ὅταν λέγῃ Ὅμηρος 'ἡ δὲ μολυβδαίνῃ ἰκέλη κτλ.' are the product of the differences between the 'constructions' of the contexts of the words concerned, or that between Hdt. III, 67, 1 οὐ γὰρ ἦν οἱ ἀσφαλὲς Καμβύσεω τετελευτηκότος φάναι τὸν Κύρου υἱὸν ἀπολωλεκέναι αὐτοχειρίῃ and 67, 2 ὁ δὲ δὴ μάγος τελευτήσαντος Καμβύσεω ἀδεῶς ἐβασίλευσε a difference between the perfect and aorist aspects. These hypotheses do not in fact survive testing, and we are constantly confronted with differences for the explanation of which we would need to draw linguistic distinctions of increasing complexity and increasingly obvious irrelevance, e.g. X. *HG*, I, 2, 16 Ἀλκιβιάδης δὲ

[1] Relevant statistics (in terms of *S*, *O* and *P* = Predicate) are to be found in Frisk, pp. 16ff.

[2] Delbrück, *Germ.* p. 10, calls the order *SV* 'normal' and *VS* 'invertiert', Frisk, pp. 39, *al.*, 'gerade Stellung' and 'Inversion'.

ἐδίωκεν ἔχων τούς τε ἱππέας καὶ τῶν ὁπλιτῶν εἴκοσι καὶ ἑκατόν, ὧν ἦρχε Μένανδρος, *An.* I, 7, 11 ἄλλοι δὲ ἦσαν ἑξακισχίλιοι ἱππεῖς, ὧν Ἀρταγέρσης ἦρχε, Th. II, 30, 1 καὶ Ἀστακόν, ἧς Εὔαρχος ἐτυράννει, λαβόντες...προσεποιήσαντο, 80, 6 Ὀρέσται δὲ χίλιοι, ὧν ἐβασίλευεν Ἀντίοχος, μετὰ Παραυαίων ξυνεστρατεύοντο. In short, the relationships *S–V* and *O–V* are in the last resort no more stable in order than the relationships illustrated in ch. I (i). Yet in recognising this fact we must also account for the statistics. What exactly do they prove?

Using throughout the classification of clauses explained in ch. II (ii), I omit from all the statistics in this section all *S–V* relationships in which *V* is εἶναι, whether copulative or existential, or copulative γίγνεσθαι.[1] I include in *O* the genitive or dative with verbs which never or rarely take an external accusative, e.g. χρῆσθαι, ἐπιθυμεῖν, and the dative of the indirect object with verbs meaning 'give', 'say', etc., where no direct object is expressed. Where any of these verbs do have an accusative object, I treat that as *O*. I exclude from *O* the neuter accusative singular or plural of an adjective without the article, e.g. κακὰ φρονεῖν, δεινὸν ποιεῖσθαι.

(ii) PREFERENTIAL WORDS

It is obvious that when *S* is an interrogative the ratio *SV*: *VS* will be very high; so will *OV*: *VO* when *O* is an interrogative.[2] We should therefore expect in general that when *S* or *O* is M^a, *SV* and *OV* will be commoner than when *S* or *O* is M^b. This expectation may be tested statistically; I give below the figures for $S=M^a$ and $O=M^a$. By '$S=M^a$' I mean that *S* is either (i) wholly composed of M^a, e.g. ἐγὼ ὁρῶ, or (ii) contains M^a and is wholly on one side of the verb or the other, e.g. τόνδε τὸν ἄνδρα ὁρῶ; cases such as τὸν ἄνδρα ὁρῶ τόνδε are excluded from these statistics. '$O=M^a$' is to be similarly interpreted. I do not regard αὐτός by itself as ever constituting *S* or *O*, and I admit πᾶς by itself as constituting *S* or *O* only when it requires the translation 'everyone' or 'everything' and forbids the translation 'all of them', 'all of us', etc.

[1] Ebeling's statistics of the copula give a picture quite different from that which is given by statistics of verbs other than the copula.

[2] Thomson analyses the logical circumstances in which interrogatives are displaced from their normal leading position.

		SV	*VS*	*OV*	*VO*
ἐγώ, etc.	Hdt.	7	1	5	2
	Lys.	9	—	2	2
	Pl.	49	9	15	3
σύ	Hdt.	5	—	—	—
	Lys.	12	—	—	—
	Pl.	40	10	—	—
οὗτος	Hdt.	21	7	28	25
	Lys.	25	—	46	7
	Pl.	21	8	70	19
ἐκεῖνος	Hdt.	2	1	1	—
	Lys.	8	1	8	1
	Pl.	2	1	2	3
αὐτός	Hdt.	2	1	—	—
	Lys.	1	—	2	—
	Pl.	1	—	3	1
ὁ αὐτός	Hdt.	—	—	6	—
	Lys.	—	—	4	—
	Pl.	1	—	1	—
ἄλλος	Hdt.	2	—	2	—
	Lys.	2	—	2	1
	Pl.	3	2	12	4
ἕτερος	Hdt.	3	—	1	—
	Lys.	2	—	4	—
ἀμφότεροι	Lys.	1	—	1	—
πολύς	Hdt.	2	—	1	—
	Lys.	4	1	19	—
	Pl.	1	—	7	1
εἷς	Hdt.	—	—	1	—
	Pl.	—	—	1	—
TOTALS	Hdt.	44	10	45	27
	Lys.	63	2	88	11
	Pl.	118	30	111	31
	Total	225	42	244	69

		SV:*VS*	*OV*:*VO*
RATIOS	Hdt.	4·4	1·67
	Lys.	31·5	8
	Pl.	3·93	3·58

As these figures accord closely with the general picture of M^a given in I (iii), so too the figures for ὅδε and πᾶς reflect the differences between authors illustrated there:

		SV	*VS*	*OV*	*VO*
ὅδε	Hdt.	—	1	1	11
	Lys.	1	—	—	1
	Pl.	7	2	8	2
πᾶς	Hdt.	—	3	7	5
	Lys.	—	—	11	1
	Pl.	7	—	8	2

(iii) ORDINARY WORDS

Let us now see what happens when *S* and *O* are M^b. I distinguish between:

(*a*) | *SV*, in which no *M* of any kind precedes *S* in the clause.

(*b*) *nSV*, in which *S* is preceded by a negative but by no other *M*.

(*c*) -*SV*, in which *S* is preceded by at least one *M* other than a negative.

So too *nVS*, -*VS*, | *OV*, etc. Clauses containing *S*, *O* and *V* will appear twice in the tables, once for their *S–V* and again for their *O–V* relationship. Thus e.g. Pl. *La.* 184D νῦν δὲ τὴν ἐναντίαν... Λάχης Νικίᾳ ἔθετο is both -*SV* and -*OV*. I give separate figures for seven of the eight types of clause defined in II (ii); *a*/*inf.* is so rare in the texts analysed that I have omitted it.

		mn.	*sb.*	*pt.**	*pt.*	*a*/*pt.*	*inf.**	*inf.*
|*SV*	Hdt.	27	15	15	14	3	—	11
	Lys.	15	12	5	6	—	—	11
	Pl.	9	15	3	4	—	6	11
nSV	Hdt.	—	—	1	1	—	—	1
	Lys.	1	1	—	—	—	—	—
	Pl.	1	1	1	—	—	—	1
-*SV*	Hdt.	5	2	3	—	—	—	1
	Lys.	3	3	1	—	—	—	2
	Pl.	3	2	2	2	—	1	1

		mn.	*sb.*	*pt.**	*pt.*	*a/pt.*	*inf.**	*inf.*
|VS	Hdt.	23	8	12	8	2	—	2
	Lys.	3	1	2	2	—	—	—
	Pl.	3	7	—	1	—	1	1
nVS	Hdt.	—	—	—	1	—	—	—
	Lys.	—	—	—	1	—	—	—
	Pl.	1	—	—	—	—	—	—
-VS	Hdt.	4	1	1	3	1	—	—
	Lys.	1	—	—	1	1	—	—
	Pl.	1	3	—	1	1	1	1
|OV	Hdt.	17	5	—	13	3	—	14
	Lys.	38	20	1	26	3	—	39
	Pl.	15	10	—	7	2	—	22
nOV	Hdt.	—	—	—	—	—	—	3
	Lys.	—	2	—	3	—	—	—
	Pl.	2	3	—	3	—	—	—
-OV	Hdt.	12	3	2	2	—	—	2
	Lys.	22	5	3	10	—	—	6
	Pl.	14	6	1	—	—	1	3
|VO	Hdt.	34	9	2	35	1	—	7
	Lys.	11	3	—	17	1	—	9
	Pl.	17	10	—	11	2	—	17
nVO	Hdt.	—	2	—	3	—	—	2
	Lys.	—	1	—	1	—	—	1
	Pl.	2	1	—	2	—	—	—
-VO	Hdt.	15	4	4	3	—	—	6
	Lys.	4	—	1	2	—	—	6
	Pl.	10	1	2	2	—	—	2

The totals for the three texts are:

	SV	*VS*	*OV*	*VO*
Hdt.	99	68	76	127
Lys.	60	12	178	57
Pl.	63	22	89	79

The differences of ratio between the four principal types of clause (omitting *pt.**, *a/pt.*, *inf.** and *a/inf.* as inadequately represented) are:

	Hdt.		Lys.		Pl.	
	SV:VS	*OV:VO*	*SV:VS*	*OV:VO*	*SV:VS*	*OV:VO*
mn.	1·19	0·59	4·75	4	2·6	1·07
sb.	1·97	0·53	16	6·75	1·8	1·58
pt.	1·25	0·37	1·5	1·95	3	0·67
inf.	3·25	1·27	∞	2·81	6·5	1·32

It appears that there is a consistent preference for *SV*, and that this preference is more marked in *inf.* than elsewhere. With that exception, the most conspicuous feature of the tables is the differences between authors.[1] These differences, however, are not consistent differences between dialects, periods and genres; authors are not even always consistent with themselves. In Hdt. VIII, 1–48, Lys. XIX (*De Aristophanis Bonis*) and Pl. *Ion*, the comparable totals are:

	SV	*VS*	*OV*	*VO*
Hdt.	75	45	85	76
Lys.	38	24	61	55
Pl.	42	21	43	33

Comparing now the ratios *SV*: *VS* and *OV*: *VO* for all six texts, we have:

	SV:VS	*OV:VO*
Hdt. III	1·46	0·6
Hdt. VIII	1·86	1·12
Lys. XII	5·0	3·12
Lys. XIX	1·58	1·11
Pl. *Laches*	2·86	1·13
Pl. *Ion*	2·0	1·30

[1] Further data illustrating authors' preferences in different types of clause may be found in Behaghel, *St. Vb.* p. 280, and in Frisk, pp. 28ff. Hermann, pp. 500f., points out that there are no structural characteristics of *sb.* which are general *IE.* 'Nachsätze' (see p. 20 n. 1) which fulfil the requirements of my argument by containing either $S = M^b$ and V or $O = M^b$ and V are too few in the texts analysed to be distinguished from other *mn.* So far as they go, they exhibit *S V*, *V S*, *O V* and *V O*.

Plato is the most consistent. Lysias shows a very much greater preference for *SV* and *OV* in XII than in XIX. Herodotus in VIII agrees with Lysias and Plato in preferring *OV*, but differs greatly from his own practice in III.

It is clear that these statistics are very far indeed from establishing for 'Classical Greek' *simpliciter* anything worth calling a syntactical rule of word order. Extended to a much greater variety of authors and texts, they would no doubt give us an interesting picture of the vagaries of individual preference—and thereby suggest with increasing force that all patterns of order which are describable in syntactical terms are secondary phenomena.

CHAPTER IV

LOGICAL DETERMINANTS

A. General Principles

(i) EMPHASIS

The fact that Greek utterances identical not merely in structure but also in content may still differ in order, the variations in structural preference between authors and between different portions of the same author's work, and the high proportion of 'abnormality' even in authors whose preferences are consistent, suggest that some, at least, of the determinants of order must be sought not inside the utterance itself, but outside it, in its relation to its context.[1] In modern spoken English such relations are expressed by modification of the tone and volume of the voice, so that two utterances which in writing are identical may be revealed in speech as standing in quite different logical relations to their contexts.[2]

These relations in Greek have sometimes been discussed in terms of 'emphasis', sometimes in terms of the distinction between 'logical subject' and 'logical predicate'. For pedagogic purposes, rough rules have been formulated in the terminology of emphasis, e.g. 'the emphatic positions in a Greek sentence are at the beginning and the end'.[3] Yet the term 'emphasis' is for a variety of reasons unsatisfactory.

(*a*) 'Emphatic' is commonly used to describe both words which are the focus of the speaker's emotion and words which are essential to the clarity of his argument.[4] Some passages of

[1] Cf. Loepfe, pp. 8, 130, Kaibel, p. 96, on the failure of purely grammatical explanations.

[2] Cf. Brugmann, *Vschd.* pp. 4f., 9ff., Richter, p. 28, on the variety of function fulfilled by tone and volume of voice.

[3] Denniston, *Pr. St.* p. 44, Delbrück, *Vgl. Synt.* pp. 110ff.

[4] Firbas, *Comm.* p. 39, uses 'emotive' to denote all kinds of 'emphasis'. Yet the distinction is vital; clear explanation and the stimulation of emotion are often incompatible; so are humour and explanation, for the humour of the unexpected requires the speaker to create a misleading expectation, and this is not a common or profitable didactic technique. Richter, p. 37, makes a fundamental distinction between 'gefühlerregende Rede' and 'berichtende Rede'.

Greek prose are designed to stimulate in the hearer pity, terror, anger, scorn or pride; the majority are not: they are designed to make the hearer understand, and the only emotion which sustains them is the determination to communicate intelligibly. The difference in purpose and circumstances between language which stimulates irrational emotion and the language of exposition is profound, but the term 'emphasis' obscures this difference.

(*b*) Emphasis is necessarily a matter of degree. There are some short utterances in which it is possible to designate one component unhesitatingly as 'emphatic' and another as 'unemphatic'; but most Greek utterances are longer and more complex. Consider for example Heraclitus, fr. 57: διδάσκαλος δὲ πλείστων Ἡσίοδος· τοῦτον γὰρ ἐπίστανται πλεῖστα εἰδέναι, ὅστις ἡμέρην καὶ εὐφρόνην οὐκ ἐγίνωσκεν· ἔστι γὰρ ἕν. If we possessed the original context of this fragment, we should probably be able to say which of the words in the first clause is less emphatic than its neighbours; but with that exception, I should find it very hard either to allocate the remaining words between the categories 'emphatic' and 'unemphatic' or to arrange them on any scale of emphasis.[1] Objections of a similar kind may be brought against all analyses of logical relationships; but we must seek, and may find, an analysis which admits of more absolutes than the concept 'emphasis' does.

(*c*) To a remarkable extent, individuals may disagree about the location of 'emphasis' in a given passage of Greek,[2] and an individual may disagree with himself on different occasions.

(*d*) These three defects of analysis in terms of 'emphasis' combine to lead us into a danger which is never far away in the study of dead languages. We suspect that there is a certain semantic difference between two alternative formulations; we find certain examples in which the difference of formulation coincides with this semantic difference; upon these examples we base a general rule; we then

[1] See p. 37 n. 1, p. 53 n. 1.

[2] Goodell, pp. 22ff., 27f., 38f., remarks on this danger. I find it impossible to agree with Ebeling's interpretation (pp. 236f.) of sentences which seem to him to illustrate his general principle, and I find much room for similar disagreement, both on principles and on their particular illustrations, with Fischer, pp. 194ff., Holwerda, p. 45, Richter, pp. 33f., Schöne, *Umstr.* pp. 171f., Meillet, pp. 365ff., Wundt, pp. 350, 368 n. 1.

translate all other examples of the alternative formulations in such a way as to make them conform to the rule; and finally we treat our translations as evidence for the validity of the rule.[1]

(ii) LOGICAL CATEGORIES

Rules defined in terms of 'logical subject' and 'logical predicate' (or 'psychological' or 'cognitional' subject and predicate, or 'determinand' and 'determinant', or 'thema' and 'rhema')[2] escape to a large extent the disadvantages of rules defined in terms of emphasis. They avoid the risk of confusion between the rational and the emotional, they leave little room for disagreement on analysis, and still less room for disagreement on questions of degree.

The essential difference between 'logical subject' and 'logical predicate' may be illustrated by taking some simple English utterance such as 'dogs bite'. Irrespective of context, the syntactical relationship between the two elements of this utterance is constant; 'dogs' is always the syntactical subject and 'bite' is always the syntactical predicate. If the context of this utterance is a discussion of the habits of dogs, syntactical subject and logical subject coincide; 'dogs' denotes the subject-matter, τὸ περὶ οὗ, τὸ ὑποκείμενον. If, on the other hand, the context is a discussion of creatures which bite, the logical classification of the elements of the utterance is the reverse of the syntactical; 'bite' becomes the logical subject, and 'dogs' the logical predicate. In English, the syntactical categories determine the order of words, the logical categories the volume of the voice.

[1] This criticism may, I think, be levelled against Barbelenet, *Etre*, pp. 63 ff., 103 f., and Ammann's semantic classification (*Unt.* II, pp. 300 ff.) of examples of αἱρεῖν and ἑλεῖν in Homer.

[2] 'Logical': Weil, pp. 14 *al.*, Holwerda, p. 24, Gardiner, p. 273, Sandmann, pp. 101 ff.; 'psychological': Gabelentz, *Weit.* pp. 129, 335, *Sprw.* pp. 365, 370, Paul, p. 236, Dittmar, p. 40; 'cognitional': Sandmann, pp. 142 ff., 245 ff.; 'determin-': Dittmar, pp. 37 ff., Richter, p. 25; 'rhema' and 'thema': Loepfe, p. 23. Firbas, *Comm.* p. 39, *WO*, p. 71, *Non-Th.* p. 171, distinguishes between 'theme' or 'communicative basis' and 'rheme' or 'communicative nucleus'. I do not imply that all these authors use all these terms synonymously; I cite them simply as examples of distinctions which are in varying degrees analogous to the grammarian's distinction between subject and predicate, but must be drawn in the light of the logical relation of an utterance to its context and are not necessarily revealed by grammatical form.

The difference between the logical categories can be described in several different ways:

(i) In the two contexts which I have postulated, the utterance 'dogs bite' is an answer to an implicit question;[1] in the first context, 'what do dogs do?', and in the second, 'which animals bite?' In each case the utterance could be reduced to the logical predicate alone; it would be laconic, but it would be intelligible; the logical subject is the element which is common to question and answer.[2]

(ii) The logical subject is what one would leave out if one were sending a telegram; the logical predicate is what one would leave in.[3]

(iii) The logical subject is the element which is expected or predicted by the hearer; the logical predicate is the element which is new, unexpected and unpredictable to him.[4]

To amplify now the concepts 'dispensable' and 'predictable':

(*a*) In speaking of a word in a given context as 'dispensable' I do not mean necessarily that it could be omitted without any grammatical adjustment of what remains; thus in saying that ἐπιθυμεῖς is logically dispensable in Ar. *Nu.* 435 τεύξει τοίνυν ὧν ἱμείρεις· οὐ γὰρ μεγάλων ἐπιθυμεῖς I recognise that its omission would make the change of μεγάλων to μεγάλα desirable.

(*b*) Words are not dispensable or predictable solely by virtue of their relation to the *verbal* context; their relation to their *material* context is also relevant.[5] In *SIG*³, 35 B a *H*ιάρōν ὁ Δεινομένεος καὶ τοὶ Συρακόσιοι τõι Δὶ Τυράν' ἀπὸ Κύμας, the word 'dedicated' is dispensed with because it can be understood from a combination of the words themselves with the nature and location of the object upon which they are inscribed.

(*c*) Whether or not dispensability and predictability are determinants of order remains to be seen; but we can say for certain that in any language whatsoever there are circumstances in which order

[1] Weil, p. 22, Gabelentz, *Sprw.* p. 366, Wundt, p. 349, Dittmar, p. 40, Gardiner, pp. 273 f., Hatcher, pp. 239 ff.

[2] Loepfe, p. 28.

[3] Cf. Gabelentz, *Sprw.* p. 366, on exclamations.

[4] Goodell, pp. 30 f., Richter, p. 13, Loepfe, p. 25, Bolinger, pp. 1118 ff.

[5] That is to say, the whole situation of speaker and hearer, or of writer and reader, must be taken into account, and not merely those aspects of the situation which are put into words. This is stressed by Brugmann, *Vschd.* pp. 13 f., Gabelentz, *Sprw.* p. 370, Richter, pp. 13, 15 ff., de Vries, p. 23, Loepfe, pp. 18, 35 f., Gardiner, *passim.*

determines predictability. In X. *HG*, 1, 2, 16 ὧν ἦρχε Μένανδρος the relative pronoun ὧν tells us nothing certain about the content of the clause which it introduces; Xenophon may, for all the hearer knows, be about to say 'of whom the majority had lost their shields'; we cannot predict ἦρχε from ὧν, and still less can we predict Μένανδρος from ἦρχε. On the other hand, in *An.* 1, 7, 11 ὧν 'Αρταγέρσης ἦρχε, given the words ὧν 'Αρταγέρσης, the following ἦρχε has a high degree of predictability, for after ὧν and a man's name the author is more likely to be going on to say 'led' or 'commanded' than anything else. Similarly in *IG*, 1^2, 865 B [*h*]όρος [τεμέ]νος 'Α[ρτεμί]δος 'Α[μαρυ]σίας, ὅρος does not tell us 'boundary of what?', nor does τεμένους tell us 'sacred land of whom?'; hence the second word is not predictable from the first, nor is the third predictable from the first two. But in 865 A *h*όρος 'Αρτεμίδος τεμένος 'Αμαρυ[σ]ίας the word τεμένους is both predictable and dispensable, for 'boundary of Artemis' can only be 'boundary of the temple/sacred land of Artemis'; compare the complete inscription *h*όρος Διός (*IG*, 1^2, 863), in which 'temple' or 'sacred land' is understood.

(*d*) The criterion of dispensability in Greek is, or can be made, a very strict one. We are entitled to say that a word in a given utterance is dispensable if we can find, preferably, an identical utterance, or, failing that, a very similar one, in the same author, or in the same place and period, in which it is actually dispensed with. Thus we can say that in 'Callias dedicated me to Athena' the words 'dedicated me' are dispensable because we have actual examples of 'Callias to Athena'.

(*e*) Dispensability and predictability are not always the same thing. Compare with ὧν ἦρχε Μένανδρος the modern English practice of writing the name of a man in brackets after the name of a ship or a military formation. By convention, the name in brackets is the name of the commander; hence in English the words 'commanded by' are dispensed with. In Greek this convention is not used, so that in ὧν 'Αρταγέρσης ἦρχε the word ἦρχε has a certain degree of predictability but is not dispensable.

(*f*) 'A certain degree' is an unavoidable qualification. A word can never be wholly predictable from the preceding words; at the best it can only be overwhelmingly likely, and more often it is predictable only in the sense that it is the most likely of a small number of feasible alternatives. Similarly, in speaking in paragraph (*d*) of 'identical...or...very similar' utterances I tacitly admitted that in one sense dispensability also may be a matter of degree.[1] Nevertheless, dispensability and predictability differ from 'emphasis' in that while admitting of degrees in a positive sense they admit of absolutes in a negative sense. I do not know what would be meant by calling a word 'absolutely emphatic'; but in any context there are words which are 'absolutely indispensable' or 'absolutely unpredictable'. So long, therefore, as certain characteristics can be wholly absent from some of the elements with which we are dealing, the risk of imprecision entailed in the fact that their presence in the remainder is a matter of degree is an acceptable risk.

The starting-point of this discussion of dispensability and predictability was the traditional distinction between 'logical subject' and 'logical predicate'. This traditional distinction is by no means coincident with the distinction between the dispensable and the indispensable or between the predictable and the unpredictable. The position is rather that when we devise examples of the simplest kind to illustrate the traditional distinction as sharply as we can these examples draw our attention to other ways of describing the logical relation between the components of an utterance and suggest the possibility that these ways may be more fundamental in character, and of a wider application, than the traditional terminology.

This possibility is realisable. In postulating two contexts for the English utterance 'dogs bite' I chose two of the same type, in which one element is 'given' by the situation or 'inherited' from what has preceded. This, however, is not the only type of context. Suppose that instead of the habits of dogs or the number of biting animals the context were concerned with the means by which animals defend themselves. In this context 'dogs' and 'bite' would receive in modern English different intonations but the same volume of voice. If we analyse this utterance in terms of dispensability and predictability, the answer is short and clear: both elements are indispensable and both are unpredictable. Yet it is customary to apply to this type of utterance also the analysis into 'logical subject' and 'logical predicate'; and most people familiar with these terms, if they were required to analyse 'dogs bite' in the context 'how do animals defend themselves?', would say that 'dogs' is logical subject and 'bite' logical predicate. But would this analysis be meaningful?

[1] Cf. Firbas, *Comm.* p. 42, *WO*, pp. 71 f., on degrees of 'communicative dynamism'; but see p. 53 n. 1 below.

In the type of utterance in which one element is 'given', the speaker is saying something (the logical predicate) *about* something else (the logical subject). There are other types of which something similar is true; a list with a heading, or a scholion with a lemma, is an utterance in which something (the list or the scholion) is 'predicated' of a 'theme' (the heading or the lemma). It is sometimes open to us to conceive a simpler and less formal utterance in this way, and to make our conception clear in our expression, e.g. 'as for John, they caught him', or 'the one that got away was John', converting, as it were, 'they caught John' into a heading 'John' and a minimal list 'they caught him', or 'John got away' into a heading 'the following got away' and a minimal list 'John'. The relation between theme and predicate has played a larger part in discussions of word order than it deserves, for the statement 'the theme precedes the predicate' is tautologous, and 'the predicate precedes the theme' self-contradictory. One can no more predicate something of a theme not yet expressed than one can 'contribute to' a discussion not yet proposed or begun. In the case of English utterances of the types 'as for *x*, *y*' and 'the one who *x* was *y*' we have formal linguistic grounds for saying that *x* is the theme. But where we have only the order *x*, *y* to guide us, we cannot infer that the speaker necessarily conceives *x* as theme; we can only say that *y* is not the theme.[1] Most actual utterances have neither theme nor predicate. Dionysius's story about Plato's attempts to find a pleasing arrangement of *R.* 327A κατέβην χθὲς εἰς Πειραιᾶ μετὰ Γλαύκωνος τοῦ Ἀρίστωνος is *bien trouvé*. No element in this sentence imposes itself as the 'theme'; and however determined we might be to analyse it as saying something about something else, we could never find cogent grounds for deciding whether it says something about yesterday, or about Socrates going to Piraeus, or about Socrates being with Glaucon.

It is arguable that attempts to analyse all utterances in terms of theme and predicate rest simply on a logical muddle, to which Aristotle's metaphors and the ambiguities of the word 'subject' in modern European languages have contributed significantly. Where the order *SP* is a syntactical rule, when the theme of some utterance conceived as theme and predicate happens to be the grammatical *S*

[1] In the English examples the syntactical structure indicates to the hearer or reader the speaker's conception of the utterance; order by itself does not.

the normal order satisfies the requirements of the relation between theme and predicate, i.e. *ThP* is expressed as *SP*. It is, however, an obvious fallacy to argue from '*ThP* is sometimes expressed as *SP*' to '*xy* always expresses *ThP*'.[1]

To use the term 'logical subject' of the given element in an utterance, of the theme in an utterance conceived by the speaker as theme and predicate, and of the element which a student of the language may choose to regard as a theme, defeats the original purpose of making a distinction between syntactical and logical categories; and it obscures the fundamental difference between dispensable and indispensable elements by applying the same term now to a dispensable element and now to an indispensable one.[2] Pl. *R.* 327 A contains five elements no one of which is predictable and no one of which is dispensable in the sense that if it were omitted it could be understood from the context.[3] If we are to retain the terms 'logical subject' and 'logical predicate' we must say that the utterance consists simply of five logical predicates; which would be a bizarre use of the word 'predicate'. For these reasons the traditional terminology seems to me inappropriate to the description of

[1] The consequence of failure to disentangle different modes of classification is reflected in, e.g., Goodell, p. 22, 'the grammatical subject is likely to be the logical subject', or Gabelentz, *Sprw.* p. 369, 'das Gehörte verhält sich zu dem weiter Erwarteten wie ein Subjekt zu seinem Prädikat', or Kieckers, *St. Vb.* pp. 132ff., who seems almost to equate 'first element', 'theme' and 'logical subject'.

[2] This is one of the two major defects (see also n. 3 below) of Loepfe's analysis, pp. 30, 51. He uses 'Thema' of the 'given' element, 'Neues Thema' of the element which is not 'given' but seems to him to have some affinity with the 'Thema'. Hence in Menander, *Epitr.* 149ff. τεθέασαι τραγῳδούς, οἶδ' ὅτι, καὶ ταῦτα κατέχεις πάντα. Νηλέα τινὰ Πελίαν τ' ἐκείνους εὗρε πρεσβύτης ἀνὴρ αἰπόλος he classifies Νηλέα. . . .ἐκείνους as 'Neues Thema'.

[3] Paul, p. 236, discussing an utterance of which no element is 'given', points out that each element could legitimately be regarded as 'predicated' of all that has preceded. Gabelentz, *Weit.* pp. 136f., discusses a news item in similar terms, but obscures the point by choosing to regard the first element as 'psychological subject', of which all the rest constitutes the 'psychological predicate'. The root of the trouble is the axiom (e.g. Ammann, *Dopp.* pp. 19f., Loepfe, p. 24) that the majority of utterances have one 'rhema' apiece. Loepfe, pp. 37f., therefore introduces the term 'Nachtrag' and analyses Pl. *Lys.* 203 A thus: ἐπορευόμην μὲν (Th.) ἐξ 'Ακαδημείας (Th.) εὐθὺ Λυκείου (Rh.) τὴν ἔξω τείχους (Ntr.) ὑπ' αὐτὸ τὸ τεῖχος (Ntr.). Thereby he throws away all the advantages which might have been gained by his otherwise perceptive and original principles of analysis.

the contents of an utterance in terms of their logical relations to their context. I realise that one ought not lightly to impose a new terminology upon a subject already overburdened with terminologies; but this consideration is outweighed by the obvious disadvantages of using terms which have already been used in the same connection in different senses.[1] I propose, then, to treat a Greek utterance as composed of elements of two logical types, 'nuclei' (symbol *N*) and 'concomitants' (symbol *C*). I call an element *N* if it is indispensable to the sense of the utterance and cannot be predicted from the preceding elements, and *C* in so far as it is deficient in either of those qualities.[2]

To describe in terms of *N* and *C* the utterances so far discussed: in the context concerned with the behaviour of dogs, 'dogs bite' is *C N*; in the context concerned with biting animals, it is *N C*; in the context concerned with defensive habits of animals, it is *N N*; and the opening sentence of the *Republic* is *N N pN pN pN*.

There is one further type of utterance which must be considered. Imagine someone saying: 'Keep clear of dogs; dogs bite.' If this utterance were written down, without the help of italics or underlining, any reader would interpret the second occurrence of 'dogs' as *C*. It could logically be replaced by 'they' (pronounced with diminished voice) or, indeed, omitted without serious loss of intelligibility. But the fact remains that when an utterance of this kind is spoken both elements *can* receive equal volume of voice. In other words, the speaker is treating 'dogs bite' as if the words belonged to a context different in type from that to which they actually belong. If I ask myself in what circumstances I would do this, I can give a definite answer; I would do it when I had in mind a contrast between dogs and other things; I should be implying 'other things may not bite, but dogs do'. Implicit antithesis would make me treat as *N* a word which it was open to me to treat as *C*. Now it is one thing to explain what one would have in mind if one intoned and stressed in a certain way some words of one's own language; it is quite another thing to demonstrate what was in the

[1] Cf. Richter, p. 11, on the desirability of a new terminology even in 1920. Sometimes the same term has been used in opposite senses; e.g. Ammann's 'Satzbasis' (*Unt.* 1, p. 13) is the opposite of Firbas's 'communicative basis'.

[2] 'Nucleus' is used by Firbas, see p. 34 n. 2 above. 'Nucleus', 'satellite' and 'concomitant' are used by Pittman, pp. 288f., with phonemic and morphemic connotations.

mind of an ancient writer.[1] If I formulate rules of order in terms of *N* and *C* and then explain away every recalcitrant example by saying that the writer must have chosen to treat *C* as *N*, I am wasting time on a grossly circular argument. Whether or not the situation is as difficult as this can only be discovered by seeing whether there is a 'normal' pattern of relationship between *N* and *C* and how far the abnormal instances can be defined and classified.

B. Concomitants

(i) TREATMENT OF CONCOMITANTS AS POSTPOSITIVES

By definition, *M* and *q* are such that when an utterance is composed of one of each they are arranged in the order *Mq*. We have seen that in early Greek the combination of two *M* with one or more *q* tended to be arranged in the order *Mq*(*q*) *M*. Can we trace a similar process in logical terms, of such a kind that the combination of *N* with *C* takes the form *N C*,[2] and of two *N* with *C* the form *N C N*? Again, we have seen the effect of a tendency in historical times to treat a clause as a pair or series of word-groups and to distribute *q* among these groups. Is there a parallel logical development resulting in the distribution of *C* over a series of word-groups each of which begins with *N*?[3]

The pair of documents which follow were inscribed at Tegea in the fifth century B.C. (*IG*, v, ii, 159). (B) was intended to replace and cancel (A), but fortunately (A) was not cancelled with such vigour as to render it illegible.

	(A)	(B)
§1.	Ξουθίαι τõι Φιλαχαίō δικάτιαι μναῖ	Ξουθίαι παρκαθέκα τõι Φιλαχαίō τȥετρακάτιαι μναῖ ἀργυρίō

[1] Brugmann, *Vschd.* pp. 4f., emphasises the essential difference between the study of spoken and of dead languages.

[2] Suggested (in different terminology) by Ammann, *Unt.* 1, pp. 20, 26f., Delbrück, *Altind.* pp. 51f

[3] The argument from analogy is in itself of limited value. The fact that in most Greek words the terminations give the spatio-temporal orientation of the stem accords with the arrangement *Mq*, where *q* gives similar orientation of *M*. Yet attempts to infer general 'Bestimmungsgesetze' from the structure of the word and to apply these to the structure of the sentence (e.g. Dittmar, pp. 37ff., Goodell, pp. 21, 34, Hirt, p. 235, Gabelentz, *Sprw.* p. 373, Bergaigne, pp. 22ff., 125ff.) do not do justice to the facts.

The words παρκαθήκα and ἀργυρίω are *C*, because they could have been omitted and understood from the material context; the demonstration of this is provided by (A), 1, where the composer thought it unnecessary to say that the money was a deposit or that it was in coined silver. The logical pattern of (B), 1 is: *N C pN*⁝*NN C*; I take τζετρακάτιαι μναῖ as a complex *N* of numeral type. Cf. *IG*, IX, i, 333 A (Locris, V B.C.), 4ff. αἴ κ' ἀδίκō(ς) συλο̃ι, τέτορες δραχμαί· αἰ δὲ πλέον δέκ' ἀμαρᾶν ἔχοι τὸ σῦλον, *h*ε̄μιόλιον ὀφλέτō ϝότι συλάσαι, *DGE*, 412 (Olympia, VI B.C.), 1 αἰ δὲ βενέοι ἐν τἰαρο̃ι, βοῖ κα θōάδοι καὶ κοθάρσι τελείαι. In the first provision of the Locrian document, the composer did not think it necessary to say that 'four drachmae' was a fine, given that the document is a law and laws are largely concerned with the specification of penalties. Therefore ὀφλέτω in the second provision and θωάδδοι in the Olympian document may be regarded as *C*; they exemplify respectively the logical patterns *N C pN* and *Nq C pN N*.[1]

The remainder of the Xuthias documents from Tegea is:

§2.	αἴ κ' αὐτὸς *h*ίκε̄,	εἰ μέν κα ζο̃ε̄,
	ἀνελέσθō.	αὐτὸς ἀνελέσθō.
§3.	αἰ δέ κ' ἀποθάνε̄ι,	αἰ δέ κα με̄̀ ζο̃ε̄,
	το̃ν τέκνōν ἔμεν,	τοὶ υἱοὶ ἀνελο̃́σθō τοὶ γνε̄́σιοι,
	ἐπεί κα πέντε ϝέτεα *h*ε̄βο̃ντι.	ἐπεί κα ἐ̄̓βάσōντι πέντε ϝέτεα.
§3a.		εἰ δέ κα με̄̀ ζο̃ντι,
		ταὶ θυγατέρες ἀνελο̃́σθō ταὶ γνε̄́σιαι.
§3b.		εἰ δέ κα με̄̀ ζο̃ντι,
		τοὶ νόθοι ἀνελο̃́σθō.
§4.	αἰ δέ κα με̄̀ γενεὰ λείπε̄ται,	εἰ δέ κα με̄̀ νόθοι ζο̃ντι,
	το̃ν ἐπιδικάτōν ἔμεν.	τοὶ 'ς ἄσιστα πόθικες ἀνελο̃́σθō.
§5.		εἰ δέ κ' ἀνφιλέγōντι,
	διαγνο̃μεν δὲ το̃̀ς Τεγεάτας	τοὶ Τεγεᾶται διαγνόντō
	κὰ τὸν θεθμόν.	κὰ τὸν θεθμόν.

In (A), 2 ἀνελέσθω is *N*; it is, in fact, a complete clause in itself. In (B), 2, on the other hand, the *N* status of ἀνελέσθω is in peril; given αὐτός, the sense of ἀνελέσθω becomes almost inevitable, and the

[1] I do not distinguish between N_1 *C* N_2 where N_1 and N_2 are syntactically interrelated (e.g. as *S* to *O* or as components of *S*) and the same arrangement where N_1 and N_2 are co-ordinated (e.g. S_1 *V* + S_2). Cf. Havers, *Spalt.*, *Hdb.* pp. 44f., Boldt, pp. 78ff., 103ff., Rass, Krause, pp. 245ff., Delbrück, *Altind.* pp. 58f.

word might therefore be regarded as dispensable because predictable. The composer has chosen, by means of the order, to give *C* status to a word not inevitably of that status. But in (B), 3–4 the composer no longer has a choice; given ἀνελέσθω in (B), 2, ἀνελώσθω in (B), 3, (B), 3a, (B), 3b and (B), 4 is necessarily *C*. When combined with a single *N*, in 3b, it follows it; combined with two *N*, in 3 and 3a, it is placed after the first *N*. In (B), 4 I take ἄσιστα πόθικες to be a complex *N*, so that the pattern is *ppNN C*.

A more complicated and sophisticated document, the First Decree of Callias (*Athenian Tribute Lists*, D 1) illustrates the same principles:

(§1) ἀποδõναι τοῖς θεοῖς τὰ χρέματα τὰ ὀφελό-μενα... — *N pN pN pN*...||

(§3) λογισάσθõν δὲ *h*οι λογισταί... — *Nq pN*...||

(§4) συναγõγε̃ς δὲ τõν λογιστõν ἐ̃ βολε̃ αὐτοκράτõρ ἔστõ. — *Nq pC pN N M'* ||

(§5) ἀποδόντõν δὲ τὰ χρέματα *h*οι πρυτάνες... — *Nq pC pN*...|
ȝε̄τέ̄σαντες τά τε πινάκια καὶ τὰ γραμ-ματεῖα... — *N pqN ppN*...||

(§6) ἀποφαινόντõν δὲ τὰ γεγραμμένα *h*οί τε *h*ιερε̃ς... — *Nq pC pqN*...||

In §4 τῶν λογιστῶν is *C* by virtue of οἱ λογισταί in §3; in §5, τὰ χρήματα is *C* by virtue of §1 and (by implication) §§2–4; in §6, τὰ γεγραμμένα is *C* by virtue of the latter part of §5. The decree goes on to provide for the creation of a new board of treasurers; it defines their essential function, and then proceeds to details:

(§9) παρὰ δὲ τõν νῦν ταμιõν καὶ τõν ἐπιστα-τõν... — *pqpN C ppN*...⁝
ἀπαριθμε̄σάσθõν καὶ ἀποστε̄σάσθõν τὰ χρέματα... — *N pN pC*...||

(§10) καὶ παραδεχσάσθõν *h*οι ταμίαι *h*οι λαχόν-τες παρὰ τõν νῦν ἀρχόντõν — *pN pC pN ppN C*||

With ἀπαριθμησάσθων καὶ ἀποστησάσθων τὰ χρήματα in §9 cf. ὁ βορέης τε καὶ ὁ χειμὼν ἐστᾶσι in the following passage of Herodotus (II, 26, 2):

εἰ δὲ ἡ στάσις ἤλλακτο τῶν ὡρέων — *pqpN N pN*||
καὶ τοῦ οὐρανοῦ — *ppN*⁝
τῇ μὲν νῦν ὁ βορέης τε καὶ ὁ χειμὼν ἐστᾶσι, — *pqN*⁝*pNq ppN C*||

ταύτῃ μὲν τοῦ νότου ἦν ἡ στάσις καὶ τῆς μεσαμβρίης,	*Nq⋮pN* M^q *pC ppN*‖
τῇ δὲ ὁ νότος νῦν ἕστηκε,	*pqpN⋮N C*‖
ταύτῃ δὲ ὁ βορέης,	*Nq⋮pN*‖
εἰ ταῦτα οὕτως εἶχε,	*pN⋮N C*‖
ὁ ἥλιος ἂν	*pNq*⋮
ἀπελαυνόμενος ἐκ μέσου τοῦ οὐρανοῦ	*N pN pN*⋮
ὑπὸ τοῦ χειμῶνος καὶ τοῦ βορέω	*ppN ppN*|
ἤϊε ἂν τὰ ἄνω τῆς Εὐρώπης	*Nq pN pN*‖
κατάπερ νῦν τῆς Λιβύης ἔρχεται,	*pN⋮pN C*‖
διεξιόντα δ' ἂν μιν διὰ πάσης Εὐρώπης	*Nqqq pN N*⋮
ἔλπομαι[1]	*N*
ποιέειν ἂν τὸν Ἴστρον	*Nq pN*‖
τάπερ νῦν ἐργάζεται τὸν Νεῖλον.	*pN C⋮pN*

Certain words in this passage are immediately identifiable as *C*: ἑστᾶσι, (ἦν) ἡ στάσις, and ἕστηκε, by virtue of the initial ἡ στάσις; ἔρχεται because of ἤιε ἄν, and ἐργάζεται because of ποιέειν ἄν; and εἶχε on grounds of dispensability. One of the commonest brachylogies in Greek is the omission, in a relative clause, particularly with περ, of a word intelligible from its occurrence in the preceding clause; Herodotus here, as often, avoids brachylogy by expressing words which could be left implicit. ὁ βορέης τε καὶ ὁ χειμών are a pair of *N* co-ordinated; so are τοῦ νότου καὶ τῆς μεσαμβρίης. In the former case the *C* is placed after the second *N*, in the latter case after the first. Towards the end of the passage, νῦν and τῆς Λιβύης are *N*; so are νῦν and τὸν Νεῖλον; in the former case the *C* ἔρχεται is placed after the second *N*, in the latter case the *C* ἐργάζεται after the first *N*. In this short passage we have four clear examples of *C* combined with two *N*. In two cases the *N* are co-ordinated; in the other two cases they are not.[2] Whether they are co-ordinated or not, the *C* may be placed either after the first *N* or after the second.

Platonic argument illustrates the same principles as legal documents and Herodotean exposition. In *Laches*, 194E Nicias expresses the view that courage is δεινῶν καὶ θαρραλέων ἐπιστήμη. After dealing with a certain amount of obstreperousness from Laches, Socrates embarks (196D) on an examination of Nicias's hypothesis, and begins with a formal statement of it: τὴν ἀνδρείαν ἐπιστήμην

[1] I have provisionally treated ἔλπομαι as *N*, but see (iii) below.

[2] See p. 42 n. 1 and v below.

φῇς δεινῶν τε καὶ θαρραλέων εἶναι: *pN N* M^q *Nq pN* M^q. In 198D he turns the argument to the discussion of ἐπιστῆμαι in general, and in 199B begins his conclusion οὐκοῦν, ὦ ἄριστε, καὶ ἡ ἀνδρεία τῶν δεινῶν ἐπιστήμη ἐστὶν καὶ θαρραλέων: *N...ppN pN C* M^q *pN*. He reminds Nicias what τὰ δεινὰ καὶ τὰ θαρραλέα are; he reminds him of the nature of ἐπιστήμη. Then: οὐ μόνον ἄρα τῶν δεινῶν καὶ θαρραλέων ἡ ἀνδρεία ἐπιστήμη ἐστίν: *N Nq pN pN pN C* M^q. The argument continues (199C): 'You have told us about a part of courage; but we were asking what courage as a whole was. Now it seems οὐ μόνον δεινῶν τε καὶ θαρραλέων ἐπιστήμη ἡ ἀνδρεία ἐστίν': *N N Nq pN N pC* M^q. My analysis here does not depend upon subjective interpretation of 'emphasis', but upon the simple test of dispensability. In 199B οὐ μόνον ἄρα, κτλ., given the preceding few lines, ἡ ἀνδρεία could not be omitted without causing confusion, but ἐπιστήμη ἐστίν could. In 199C the reverse is the case.

With the exception of εἶχε in Herodotus's εἰ ταῦτα οὕτως εἶχε, all the words which I have so far treated as *C* have been words 'given' by the verbal or material context. There is in addition a common type of *C* (εἶχε is an example) which is dispensable in so far as the word-group which contains it could be rephrased to convey the essential meaning without it. An easily applied test is to substitute *q* or M^q. Thus in Pl. *Grg.* 470D Εὐδαίμων οὖν σοι δοκεῖ εἶναι ἢ ἄθλιος; Οὐκ οἶδα, ὦ Πῶλε, οὐ γάρ πω συγγέγονα τῷ ἀνδρί, the words τῷ ἀνδρί are *pC* because they could be replaced by the *q* αὐτῷ. Cf. κεῖται in two passages of Herodotus:

VII, 198, 2	(...ἄλλος ποταμὸς) τῷ οὔνομα κεῖται Δύρας	*pN C N*
	=τῷ οὔνομά ἐστι Δύρας	*pN* M^q *N*
	=τῷ οὔνομα Δύρας	*pN N*
200, 2	(κώμη τε ἔστι) τῇ οὔνομα Ἀνθήλη κεῖται	*pN N C*
	=τῇ οὔνομα Ἀνθήλη ἐστί	*pN N* M^q
	=τῇ οὔνομα Ἀνθήλη	*pN N*

In cases to which the test of substitution is inapplicable there is room for much doubt and disagreement, according to one's view of the extent to which the sense conveyed by the omission of the alleged *C* falls short of the 'essential' sense. For example in Pl. *Euthyphro*, 2A τὰς ἐν Λυκείῳ καταλιπὼν διατριβὰς ἐνθάδε νῦν διατρίβεις there is antithesis between ἐν Λυκείῳ and ἐνθάδε and between καταλιπών and νῦν; these are certainly *N*, and διατρίβεις is certainly *C*; but I may not command agreement in suggesting that διατριβάς is also *C* (τὰς ἐν Λυκείῳ...διατριβάς being replaceable by τὸ Λύκειον), so that the logical structure of the whole utterance is *ppN*⁝*N C*|*N*⁝*N C*. Cf. D. LIV, 3 ἡμεῖς δ' ὥσπερ ἐνθάδ' εἰώθειμεν, οὕτω διήγομεν καὶ ἔξω=*N*(=*M*ᵃ) *q*⁝*pN C*||*N*(=*M*ᵃ) *C*⁝*pN*, in which εἰώθειμεν might plausibly be regarded as *N*; it is its subordination to the strong antithesis ἐνθάδε/ἔξω which gives it its flavour of *C*.

The passages already analysed have shown the analogy between *M*⁝*Mq* and *N*⁝*N C*, and I add one further example of the 'distribution' of *C*, Lys. I, 15–16:

προσέρχεταί μοί τις πρεσβῦτις ἄνθρωπος	*Nqq N C*|
ὑπὸ γυναικὸς ὑποπεμφθεῖσα...	*pN N*...||
αὕτη δὲ (*sc.* ἡ γυνή)...	*N*(=*M*ᵃ)*q*...||
προσελθοῦσα οὖν μοι	*Nqq*⁝
ἐγγὺς ἡ ἄνθρωπος τῆς οἰκίας τῆς ἐμῆς ἐπιτηροῦσα...	*N pC pN pN N*|
'Εὐφίλητε', ἔφη,....	*N C*...

Here the *C* ἡ ἄνθρωπος is placed after the leading word of the second word-group of a sentence in the manner of e.g. the *q* μοι in D. XXI, 26 οὑναντίος ἧκεν ἂν εὐθύς μοι λόγος.

(ii) CONCOMITANT GROUPS

Naturally the *C* element in a clause may be more than a single word. The simplest type of complex *C*, like the simplest of complex *N*, is a pair of words which together constitute a familiar expression and are rarely separated, but a clause may also contain a succession of *C* which all have similar logical relations to the preceding clause(s) but are not united by any other common factor. Both types are illustrated by §§ 10–12 of the First Decree of Callias:

(§ 10) ...καὶ ἐν στέλει ἀναγραφσάντōν μιᾶι ἅπαντα...	*ppN N N N*...||
(§ 11) καὶ τὸ λοιπὸν ἀναγραφόντōν *hoι* αἰεὶ ταμίαι ἐς στέλēν	*ppN C pN C pC*||
καὶ λόγον διδόντōν τōν τε ὄντōν χρēμάτōν καὶ τōν προσιόντōν τοῖς θεοῖς...	*pN N pqN C ppNC p*||

(§12) καὶ ἐκ Παναθēναίōν ἐς Παναθέναια τὸλ λόγον διδόντōν... *ppN pN pCC*

In §12 ἐκ Παναθηναίων ἐς Παναθήναια is a complex *N* of familiar type; τὸν λόγον διδόντων is a comparable type of *C*. In §11 the *N* are τὸ λοιπόν and οἱ αἰεί; ταμίαι and ἐς στήλην are both *C* by virtue of what has preceded, but the *C* status of each of them is independent of that of the other and of ἀναγραφόντων.

Three literary passages illustrate the treatment of *C* groups; they are arranged in ascending order of magnitude:

(*a*) *Euthyphro*, 8E

πράξεώς τινος πέρι διαφερόμενοι	*Nqq N*|
οἱ μὲν δικαίως φασὶν αὐτὴν πεπρᾶχθαι,	*Nq*⁝*N Cq C*||
οἱ δὲ ἀδίκως	*Nq*⁝*N*

Here φασίν is strictly speaking M^q in character, and the word-group which I have analysed as *N Cq C* is therefore on the borderline of the category '*C* group'; it admits of the analysis $N\ M^q q\ C$.

(*b*) *Chrm.* 164D

καὶ συμφέρομαι τῷ ἐν Δελφοῖς ἀναθέντι τὸ τοιοῦτον γράμμα.	*pN ppN N pN N*||
καὶ γὰρ τοῦτο οὕτω μοι δοκεῖ τὸ γράμμα ἀνακεῖσθαι, ὡς...	*pqN*⁝*Nq C pC C*|*p*...

The word-group headed by the *N* οὕτω stands essentially in the same relation to τοῦτο as may be seen in the much simpler Herodotean clause εἰ ταῦτα⁝οὕτως εἶχε. The first *C* of the group, δοκεῖ, is, like φασίν, a word of special status (see section (iii)).

(*c*) Hdt. 1, 1, 1

(...τά τε ἄλλα καὶ δι' ἣν αἰτίην ἐπολέμησαν ἀλλήλοισι.)

Περσέων μέν νυν οἱ λόγιοι	*Nqq pN*⁝
Φοίνικας αἰτίους φασὶ γενέσθαι τῆς διαφορῆς	*N C C C pC*

Here again φασί and γενέσθαι are words of special status, classifiable as M^q, so that the word-group Φοίνικας...διαφορῆς may be analysed as $N(=M^b)\ C(=M^b)\ C(=M^q)\ C(=M^q)\ pC(=M^b)$, and is clearly modelled upon *M*⁝*Mqq M*.

(iii) TREATMENT OF CONCOMITANTS AS PREPOSITIVES

The analogy between *Mq M* and *N C N* suggests the possibility of a similar analogy between *pM* and *C N*. There are, I believe, certain categories of word which are commonly treated as if they were *p*. Consider, for example, Hdt. III, 81, 2:

καίτοι τυράννου ὕβριν φεύγοντας ἄνδρας	*pqN N N C*⁝
ἐς δήμου ἀκολάστου ὕβριν πεσεῖν	*pN N C N* (⁝?)
ἐστι οὐδαμῶς ἀνασχετόν.	ἐστι *N N* ‖

What is the status of ἐστι here? Is it, as M^q, to be compared to *q* immediately following a word-group which it is nowadays customary to mark off by commas (ch. II, (i), (I), p. 13)? Or is it wrong to suppose that there is any kind of pause in the voice after πεσεῖν? The latter question, at least, cannot be asked about III, 82, 1:

ἐμοὶ δὲ τὰ μὲν εἶπε Μεγάβυζος	*Nq* ‖ *pq* εἶπε *N*⁝
ἐς τὸ πλῆθος ἔχοντα	*ppN C* ‖
δοκέει οὐκ ὀρθῶς λέξαι.	δοκέει *NN C* ‖

Both εἶπε and δοκέει are obviously *C* in character, since they are logically dispensable; yet both of them here are the first *M* of a clause. Cf. also Hp. *Carn.* 4, 3:

εἴ τις ἐθέλοι ὀπτᾶν νευρώδεά τε καὶ κολλώδεα καὶ τἄλλα δέ,	*pq* ἐθέλοι *N Nq pN pNq* ‖
τὰ μὲν ἄλλα ταχὺ ὀπτᾶται,	*pqN*⁝ *N C* ‖
τὰ δὲ νευρώδεά τε καὶ κολλώδεα οὐκ ἐθέλει ὀπτᾶσθαι...	*pqNq pN*⁝ *N C C*... ‖
τὸ δὲ πιότατον καὶ λιπαρὸν τάχιστα ὀπτᾶται.	*pqN pN*⁝ *N C* ‖

The passage exemplifies the same logical principles as that of Herodotus on the path of the sun, with the single exception of ἐθέλοι; cf. *ibid.* 19, 6 εἰ δέ τις βούλεται καὶ τοῦτο ἐλέγξαι, κτλ., where βούλεται is as insignificant for the essential sense of the passage as ἐθέλοι in 4, 3.

It would therefore seem possible that words meaning 'think', 'seem', 'want', 'be willing', 'say', and 'be', when there is no significant antithesis between thinking and saying, wishing and doing, being and becoming, or appearance and reality, can be treated as if they were *p*.[1] This is by no means the full story of the behaviour of εἶναι (see section (iv)), but it offers an explanation of the very common type of clause νομίζων οὕτως ἂν ἄριστα πρᾶξαι, in which *q* is placed not after the word meaning 'thinking', 'knowing', 'hoping', etc., but after the next *M*. It is noteworthy that these words are dispensable in the sense that they could be replaced by ὡς with a participial construction or simply by an accusative and infinitive construction.[2]

(iv) PREFERENTIAL TREATMENT OF CONCOMITANTS

Demonstrative words are often logically *C*, but they are exempt from the treatment which I have described in sections (i) and (ii); their role as M^a may take precedence over their logical category. Thus we find in the First Decree of Callias:

(§7) ταμίας δὲ ἀποκυαμεύεν τούτōν τō̃ν χρēμάτōν...	*Nq N C pC* ...‖
(§8) *h*οῦτοι δὲ ταμιευόντōν ἐμ πόλει...	M^a*q C pN*...‖

οὗτοι in §8 is as dispensable, logically speaking, as τούτων in §7, but is nevertheless given precedence. This treatment of demonstrative words is extended to words which are in explicit antithesis;[3] the nature of the extension may be seen in many passages of Herodotus's catalogue of Xerxes' army, e.g.:

VII, 62, 2–63

Κίσσιοι δὲ...μιτρηφόροι ἦσαν.	*Nq*...*N* M^q‖
Κισσίων δὲ ἦρχε 'Ανάφης...	*Cq N N*...‖
'Ασσύριοι δὲ...ἐγχειρίδια...εἶχον...	*Nq*...*N*...*C*...‖
οὗτοι δὲ ὑπὸ μὲν Ἑλλήνων ἐκαλέοντο Σύριοι...	M^a*q*⁝*pqN N N*...‖
ἦρχε δέ σφεων 'Οτάσπης.	*Nqq N*‖

[1] Firbas, *Comm.* pp. 45 f.

[2] Fraenkel, *Kolon*, pp. 327ff., treats νομίζων, ἡγούμενος, etc. in such utterances as 'Kurzkola'.

[3] Demonstratives often imply antithesis, but their treatment as M^a does not depend on their antithetical element; cf. σὺ δὲ = $M^a q$ in cases where antithesis is ruled out, e.g. Hdt. III, 69, 3 καὶ ἢν μὲν φαίνηται ἔχων ὦτα, νόμιζε σεωυτὴν Σμέρδι τῷ Κύρου συνοικέειν, ἢν δὲ μὴ ἔχων, σὺ δὲ τῷ μάγῳ Σμέρδι.

73–4, 1

Φρύγες δὲ ἀγχοτάτω τῆς Παφλαγονικῆς σκευὴν εἶχον... — *Nq⁝NpN C C...||*

οἱ δὲ Φρύγες...ἐκαλέοντο Βρίγες... — *pqC...N N...||*

᾿Αρμένιοι δὲ κατά περ Φρύγες ἐσεσάχατο... — *Nq⁝pqN C...||*

τούτων συναμφοτέρων ἦρχε ᾿Αρτόχμης... — *M^a N N N...||*

Λυδοὶ δὲ ἀγχοτάτω τῆς ῾Ελληνικῆς εἶχον ὅπλα... — *Nq⁝NpN C C||*

οἱ δὲ Λυδοὶ Μηίονες ἐκαλεῦντο τὸ πάλαι... — *pqC⁝N C pN...||*

From the point of view of dispensability, there is no difference between the *q* σφεων in ἦρχε δέ σφεων and the demonstratives οὗτοι and τούτων in οὗτοι...ἐκαλεῦντο and τούτων...ἦρχε, but the writer has chosen to use demonstratives in the two latter cases; he could have chosen otherwise. Equally, there is no logical difference between σφεων and Κισσίων, or between οἱ δὲ Φρύγες or οἱ δὲ Λυδοί and the third person plural termination of the verb; but the writer has chosen to cast his account of the Persian contingents in the form of a list in which each item is explicitly contrasted with what has preceded and what is to follow. 'Catalogue style', in which the initial word of an item may be a demonstrative or treated as a demonstrative, is the most obvious type of extended explicit antithesis.[1] A similar preferential treatment of *C* appears in shorter antitheses, e.g. Hdt. II, 22, 1:

λέγει γὰρ οὐδ' αὕτη οὐδέν, — *C(=p?) q pN N|*

φαμένη τὸν Νεῖλον ῥέειν ἀπὸ τηκομένης χιόνος, — *C(=p) pN N pN N||*

ὃς ῥέει[2] μὲν ἐκ Λιβύης διὰ μέσων Αἰθιόπων, — *pCq⁝pN pN N||*

ἐκδιδοῖ δὲ ἐς Αἴγυπτον. — *Nq⁝pN||*

Related to antithesis is the preferential treatment of a word in rejecting someone else's argument,[3] e.g. Hdt. II, 20, 2–3:

τῶν ἡ ἑτέρη μὲν λέγει — *ppNq C⁝*

τοὺς ἐτησίας ἀνέμους εἶναι αἰτίους πληθύειν τὸν ποταμόν... — *pNN M^q C⁝C pC*

[1] Th. VI, 43 is a good example of 'catalogue' style.

[2] It must, however, be observed that there is a logical affinity between ῥεῖ, in describing the course of a river, and the usage of ἔστι discussed below (p. 52); cf. Kieckers, *St. Vb.* pp. 58f.

[3] This is on—or over—the boundary of emotive utterance; cf. the scornful repetition in Ar. *Lys.* 430ff. μηδὲν ἐκμοχλεύετε...τί δεῖ μοχλῶν; οὐ γὰρ μοχλῶν δεῖ, κτλ.

πολλάκις δὲ ἐτησίαι μὲν οὐκ ὦν ἔπνευσαν, $Nq \vdots Cq \vdots Nq\ C \|$
ὁ δὲ Νεῖλος τωὐτὸ ἐργάζεται. $pqN \vdots N\ C \|$
πρὸς δὲ εἰ ἐτησίαι αἴτιοι ἦσαν, $Nq \vdots pC\ C\ M^q \|$
χρῆν καὶ τοὺς ἄλλους ποταμούς, $C(=p)\ ppN\ C \|$
ὅσοι τοῖσι ἐτησίῃσι ἀντίοι ῥέουσι, $ppC\ N\ C \|$
ὁμοίως πάσχειν καὶ κατὰ ταὐτὰ τῷ Νείλῳ. $N\ C\ ppN\ pN \|$

The degree of implicit antithesis involved in such an argument is almost the furthest that we can trace the influence, *via* explicit antithesis and 'catalogue style', of the preferential treatment of demonstratives. We are already passing into the sphere of influence of a different phenomenon, the preferential treatment of words which have some emotional force—among which I would class the M^a πολύς and πᾶς, in which there is necessarily a degree of emotion absent, for example, from ἔνιοι and μέρος.

A different category of preferential *C* is indicated by the relation between § 1 and § 2 of the First Decree of Callias:

(§ 1) ἀποδõναι τοῖς θεοῖς τὰ χρέματα... $N\ pN\ pN \ldots \|$
(§ 2) ἀποδιδόναι δὲ ἀπὸ τõν χρε̄μάτõν ἃ ἐς ἀπόδοσίν ἐστι τοῖς θεοῖς ἐφσε̄φισμένα $Cq\ ppC \| ppN\ M^q\ pC\ N \|$

The explanation of this phenomenon is as follows. It often happens that in a compound word one element is *N* and the other element *C*; this is true of οὐδείς, οὐκέτι, etc., e.g. in Hdt. III, 119, 6:

ἀνὴρ μὲν ἄν μοι ἄλλος γένοιτο, εἰ δαίμων ἐθέλοι, $Nqqq \vdots N\ C \| pN\ N \|$
καὶ τέκνα ἄλλα, εἰ ταῦτα ἀποβάλοιμι, $pN\ C \| pN\ N \|$
πατρὸς δὲ καὶ μητρὸς οὐκέτι μευ ζωόντων $Nq\ pN \vdots Nq\ N |$
ἀδελφεὸς ἂν ἄλλος οὐδενὶ τρόπῳ γένοιτο. $Nq\ C \vdots N\ C\ C \|$

It is true also of compound verbs, as in D. XXI, 32:

ἂν μὲν τοίνυν ἰδιώτην ὄντα τιν' αὐτῶν ὑβρίσῃ τις... $pqqN\ M^q qq\ Nq \|$
γραφὴν ὕβρεως[1]...φεύξεται, $N\ N \ldots C \|$
ἐὰν δὲ θεσμοθέτην, ἄτιμος ἔσται καθάπαξ. $pqN \| N\ M^q\ N \|$
διὰ τί; ὅτι τοὺς νόμους ἤδη $pN \| ppN\ N$
ὁ τοῦτο ποιῶν προσυβρίζει. $pN\ C\ N$

[1] ὕβρεως is not, I think, *C*, for γραφὴν ὕβρεως is balanced by δίκην κακηγορίας.

—where προσυβρίζει is analysable into *N* προσ- and *C* -υβρίζει. *A fortiori*, a preposition in a complex of preposition with noun or pronoun may be *N*; and so it is in ἀπὸ τῶν χρημάτων above.

But if a preposition or an element in a compound word may have *N* status, so may a termination or any form which belongs to a system of forms. For instance in D. XXI, 122 τίς ὁμοία τῇ τούτου γέγον' ἢ γένοιτ' ἂν πονηρία; the *N* element in γένοιτ' ἄν is not the stem γεν- but the mood index with the *q* ἄν. Here, and in expressions such as ἔστι καὶ ἔσται, ἐδόκει καὶ δοκεῖ, etc., the meaning is indicated in English (but not in all modern European languages) by diminished volume of voice on the repetition of the verb stem and augmented volume on the auxiliary, *can*, *would*, *did*, etc. English 'emphasis' may reliably be employed in translating passages such as Hdt. III, 64, 2 μαθὼν δὲ ὡς μάτην ἀπολωλεκὼς εἴη τὸν ἀδελφεόν, ἀπέκλαιε Σμέρδιν· ἀποκλαύσας δὲ καὶ περιημεκτήσας τῇ ἁπάσῃ συμφορῇ, ἀναθρῴσκει ἐπὶ τὸν ἵππον...καί οἱ ἀναθρῴσκοντι ἐπὶ τὸν ἵππον τοῦ κολεοῦ τοῦ ξίφεος ὁ μύκης ἀποπίπτει. ἀποκλαύσας δέ virtually=εἶτα, and ἀναθρῴσκοντι virtually=ἐν τούτῳ, requiring the translations '*after* he had wept...' and '*while* he was jumping up...', and exhibiting a certain affinity between this class of preferential *C* and the preferential demonstratives.[1] The class, however, includes phenomena which are not demonstrative in character and cannot be translated by English demonstratives. The verb εἶναι is sometimes used by Herodotus as a signal that an item of general rather than historical information is being given, e.g. IV, 158, 2 καὶ τὸν κάλλιστον τῶν χώρων ἵνα...μὴ ἴδοιεν,...νυκτὸς παρῆγον. ἔστι δὲ τῷ χώρῳ τούτῳ οὔνομα Ἴρασα, ctr. *ibid.* 182, 1 κολωνός τε ἁλός ἐστι ὅμοιος τῷ Ἀμμωνίῳ καὶ ὕδωρ, καὶ ἄνθρωποι περὶ αὐτὸν οἰκέουσι· τῷ δὲ χώρῳ τούτῳ οὔνομα Αὔγιλά ἐστι. In both these cases alike the English-speaker would increase the volume of voice on 'name' ('the *name* of this place...') and not on any word which could be regarded as a translation of ἐστι.[2]

ἀποδιδόναι in the Decree of Callias belongs to this category. The aorist infinitive ἀποδοῦναι in § 1 prescribes the act; the imperfective ἀποδιδόναι is the signal that a detail about the act is being prescribed, and the next words ἀπὸ τῶν χρημάτων, where ἀπό is *N*, show that it is the *source* of the money which is being prescribed.

[1] Cf. Firbas, *Comm.* p. 42 n. 25.

[2] Bloch, pp. 243 ff., Wackernagel, *Dicht.* pp. 18 ff.

Cf. *IG*, II², 16 (Athens, 394 B.C.), 10ff. ὀμόσα[ι δὲ 'Αθηναίων μὲν] τὸς στρατηγὸ[ς...καὶ τὸς ἱ]ππέας, 'Ερετριέων δὲ τ[ὸς στρατηγὸς καὶ] τὴν βολὴν...[... καὶ τὰς ἄλλας] ἀρχάς·...ὀμνύναι δὲ τὸν νόμιμ[ον ὅρκον ἑκατέρο]ς τὸν παρὰ σφίσιν αὐτοῖς.

C. NUCLEI

(i) SERIES

So far we have been concerned with the relation between *N* and *C*. A less tractable problem is raised by clauses which contain two or more *N*. Where both *N* are M^b, what determines their order? To speak of an order of importance is unhelpful, since it is rarely possible to form any opinion of the comparative importance of the different *N* in the same clause.[1]

Certain Attic boundary-inscriptions of late fifth-century date are illuminating:

IG, I², 897 δẹῦρ̣' ['Ελε]υσινίōν [τρ]ιττὺς τελ[ε]υτᾶι, Περαιōν δὲ τριττὺς ἄρχεται.

Ibid. 899 [δ]εῦρ' 'Επạ[κ]ρ̣έōν τριττὺς τελευτᾶι, Θριασίōν δὲ ἄρχεται τριττύς.

SEG, x, 374]τ[ριττὺς τ]ε⟨λ⟩ε[υτᾶι, Παλ]λēν[έōν δ]ὲ̣ ἄρχετ[αι τ]ριττύς.

IG, I², 898 [δ]εῦρε Πα[ι]ανιōν τριττὺς τελευτᾶι, ἄρχεται δὲ Μυρρινοσίōν τριττύς.

The first member of the antithesis is arranged uniformly in all cases; the name of the trittys, followed by the word τριττύς, followed by τελευτᾷ. The structure of the second member varies. The two *N* in it are the name of the trittys and ἄρχεται, and these may occur in either of their two possible orders. τριττύς is here *C*, and may be attached to either *N*, giving the two patterns *N C N* and *N N C*.

It thus appears that when two members of the same syntactical structure and similar content are in antithesis, the second member may or may not be arranged in the same order as the first. When it

[1] Firbas, *Comm.* p. 42 insists on the need to discover the relative importance of all the elements of an utterance, and speaks (*Non-Th.* pp. 171f.) of a 'transitional status' between 'rheme' and 'theme'. I do not feel able to do more than point out, in a given example, which elements have some degree of *C* status, and would prefer to leave all other questions of 'importance' alone.

is not, the order of the antithetical pair as a whole is given the technical term 'chiasmus', and may be symbolised $(xy)\,(y'x')$. The fact that boundary-stones may be chiastic shows that chiasmus is not necessarily a literary embellishment.[1] Cf. *IG*, XII, v, 593 (Iulis, V B.C.), 14ff. ἀποραίνεν τὴν οἰκίην ἐλεύθερον θαλάσσηι πρῶτον, ἔπειτα δὲ ὑσώπωι οἰκέτην ἐμβάντα, *DGE*, 179 (Gortyn, V B.C.), 9ff. μηδὲ τὰ τᾶς γυναικὸς τὸν ἄνδρα ἀποδόθαι μηδ' ἐπισπένσαι, μηδ' υἱὺν τὰ τᾶς ματρός.

Less conspicuous than chiasmus, but related to it, is the series of the type $(xy)+(x'y')+(y''x'')+(y'''x''')$ ..., in which the two members of each pair are arranged in the same order, but each pair may differ in order from the preceding pair. The following passage is taken from one of the more artless speeches of the Demosthenic corpus, [D.] XLVII, 6f.:

ἣν δ' ἐγὼ μὲν ἠξίωσα παραλαμβάνειν,
Θεόφημος δὲ προὐκαλέσατο παραδοῦναι,
ὡς οὗτοί φασιν,
τὸ δὲ σῶμ' οὐδεὶς εἶδε παρόν,...
ἐμαρτύρησαν δ' οἱ μάρτυρες οὗτοι
ὡς ἐθέλοι παραδοῦναι Θεόφημος
καὶ πρόκλησιν προκαλοῖτο,
ᾠήθησαν δ' οἱ δικασταὶ
ἀληθῆ εἶναι τὴν μαρτυρίαν,
φεύγειν δ' ἐμὲ τὸν ἔλεγχον...,
πῶς οὐκ ἀναγκαῖόν ἐστιν
τούτους τοὺς μάρτυρας τὰ ψευδῆ μεμαρτυρηκέναι;

In the first antithesis (ἐγὼ μέν, κτλ.) Θεόφημος δέ, προὐκαλέσατο and παραδοῦναι are placed in the second member in positions corresponding to ἐγὼ μέν, ἠξίωσα and παραλαμβάνειν in the first; in the third member τὸ δὲ σῶμα corresponds to ἐγὼ μέν and Θεόφημος δέ in position and in morphological category, though its syntactical role is different. In the second antithesis (ἐμαρτύρησαν δέ, κτλ.), the verb ᾠήθησαν δέ occupies the same position in the second member as the verb ἐμαρτύρησαν δέ in the first, and the subject-noun οἱ δικασταί the same as the subject-noun οἱ μάρτυρες οὗτοι. In the third antithesis (ἀληθῆ, κτλ.) the predicates ἀληθῆ εἶναι and φεύγειν δέ take first place in their respective members.

[1] Schick, pp. 370f., Leumann, pp. 797f., Delbrück, *Altind.* pp. 61f.

The fact that one cannot predict when a Greek will employ chiasmus in antithesis is a particular case of a more general phenomenon: one cannot predict at what point, in a series of members of similar or identical structure and content, the internal arrangement of the members will be changed.

There is a large class of utterances which is not as a rule mentioned in discussions of word order but is nevertheless highly relevant to this matter of series; I mean lists, especially lists of payments. For example, each item in the first Athenian Tribute-List conveys two pieces of information: the name of the city which has paid, and the ἀπαρχή of the amount which it has paid. Throughout the list, the name of the city is placed first and the amount second. In the next list, however, the order is reversed, and it remains so in all the other extant lists. The relevance of facts of this kind to the multinuclear clause may appear from consideration of some passages (*SIG*³, 241 A) from the accounts of the commissioners in charge of the reconstruction of the temple at Delphi in the fourth century. The entries made in the first part of the accounts for 356 (*SIG*³, 241 A, 4ff.), under the rubric ἔδωκε ἁ πόλις, are of a pattern which is normal throughout this series of documents. The name of the recipient is given first; then the goods or services for which the payment was made; then the amount of the payment, e.g. Πασίωνι ἰσχεγάου μνᾶς δέκα...Ἁρμοδίωι χαλκεῖ δεσμῶν μνᾶς ἕξ. In the latter part of the accounts of 356, however, there is a list of entries in which the order is changed, the goods or services being specified first and the recipient second, e.g. μαχανώματος Χαιρόλαι μνᾶς τέτορας· βολίμου εἰσφορᾶς δραχμαὶ τρεῖς, ἡμιωβέλιον· πὸτ τὸ μαχάνωμα λίθων τομᾶς Θεογένει δραχμαὶ πέντε, κτλ. The rubric which introduces this series is ἀπὸ τούτου ἀνάλωμα. Yet the change in order can hardly be related to the change in rubric, for the composer seems not to have realised at first the grammatical consequences of the new rubric; he wrote μνᾶς τέτορας in the accusative, as if under the rubric ἔδωκε ἁ πόλις, and only in the second item passed to the appropriate nominative (a confusion which occurs elsewhere in this series of documents). The abnormality of the order is in fact matched by the abnormality of the circumstances in which these payments were made. The document itself states: μετὰ τὸν λογισμόν, παρεόντων τῶν βουλευτᾶν, ἐπέταξαν τοὶ ναοποιοὶ...ἀργύριον δόμεν ποτὶ τὰ ἔργα τὰ ἐν Κορίνθωι...κεφάλωμα τοῦ ἔλαβον μετὰ τὸν λογισμὸν οἱ Κορίνθιοι ναοποιοὶ καὶ ὁ Σικυώνιος μνᾶς δεκαοκτώ. The explanation, I think, is this. The draft record of the expenditure at Corinth was presumably made not by the man who drew up the record of expenditure at Delphi, but by the Corinthian commissioners. Their arrangement differed from that adopted by the recorder of expenditure at Delphi; given a free choice whether to name the recipient before the service or the service before the recipient, the Delphian made one choice and the Corinthians made another. When the Delphian came to incorporate the Corinthian draft record into the final record, although the arrangement differed from his own, he did not think it worth-while to alter it into conformity with his own.

The important aspects of this case are: first, that in utterances of exactly similar nature and identical structure, the *N* can be differently arranged by different individuals; secondly, that one individual may adhere so consistently to one of two or more alternative arrangements that he gives it the status of a formula; and thirdly, that the formulae adopted by different individuals are nevertheless equivalent in the sense that an individual does not regard someone else's formula as incorrect.

(ii) FORMULAE

Utterances which contain a *S–V* or *O–V* relationship are no less susceptible of conversion into formulae than those which do not. Compare the formulae of the prescript of an Attic decree with the equivalent formulae of Argive decrees:[1]

(1) ἔδοξε τῇ βουλῇ καὶ τῷ δήμῳ	ἁλιαίᾳ ἔδοξε τελείᾳ
(2) ὁ δεῖνα ἐγραμμάτευε	γροφεὺς βωλᾶς ὁ δεῖνα
(3) ὁ δεῖνα ἐπεστάτει	ἀϝρήτευε ὁ δεῖνα
(4) ὁ δεῖνα εἶπε	ἔλεξε ὁ δεῖνα

The two states differ radically and consistently. In (1), Athens says 'decided by the Assembly', Argos 'by the Assembly decided'; in (2)–(4), Athens puts *S* before *V*, Argos *V* before *S*. Probably in each state the three formulae (2), (3) and (4) influenced and sustained each other; but in neither state did any of the three influence the position of *V* in (1). I would infer from this that the fact that ἔδοξε and ἐγραμμάτευε are both *V* did not suffice to make the

[1] *SEG*, XIII, 239 and *DGE*, 83 B, 23 ff. are the oldest examples (respectively early and mid fifth century B.C.) of the Argive formulae, which were still in use in the second century B.C. (e.g. *DGE*, 99, 2 ff.).

Athenian or the Argive regard ἔδοξε τῇ βουλῇ, κτλ. and ὁ δεῖνα ἐγραμμάτευε as utterances of similar structure.

The interaction of formulae can be followed in greater detail in the prescripts and subscripts of the Athenian Tribute-Lists. The factor common to all, which I omit, is ἐπὶ τῆς ἀρχῆς (with or without an ordinal numeral), to which ᾗ refers.

ATL 2, 1 *h*ε͂ι Λ[έο̄ν ἐγραμμάτευε?
3, 1 *h*]ε͂ι Διό[τ]ιμος ἐγραμ[μάτευε]

Since it was common practice to identify a board by naming its secretary—this identification, and not a desire to give interesting information about what Leon and Diotimus were doing, is the point of naming the secretary—ᾗ followed by a name makes ἐγραμμάτευε predictable and therefore *C*. This interpretation is supported by lists 4–8, where the secretary's demotic is added:

4, 1 *h*[ε͂ι ....]λε͂ς ἐγραμμά[τευε *h*α]λιμόσιος
5, 1 *h*[ε͂ι .... ἐγραμμ]άτευ[ε *H*α]λαιεύ[ς]
7, 1 *h*]ε͂ι Μενέτ[ιμο]ς ἐγρα[μμάτ]ευε Λαμ[πτρεύς
8, 2f. *h*ε͂ι Διοδ[ε͂ς ἐγραμμάτευε Π]αιονί[δε͂ς

The pattern *N C N* reminds us of dedication formulae, in which ἀνέθηκε is *C*. The situation in list 13 is very different:

13, 1f. [*h*ε͂ι Χαλ]κιδεὺς Μελιτεὺ[ς ἐγραμμάτευε Δ]ο[ρ]ύφιλος Ἰκαριεὺς *h*ελλε̄νοταμίας ε͂̓ν Σά[τυρος] Λευκονοιεὺς συνε[γραμμάτευε]

Here not only the secretary is named, but also the eponym of the board and the co-secretary. The fact that others besides the secretary are named automatically confers *N* status on ἐγραμμάτευε because it becomes antithetical; hence Χαλκιδεὺς Μελιτεὺς ἐγραμμάτευε is *N N N*. I am not arguing simply that ἐγραμμάτευε *must* be interpreted as *N because* of the change in order; for lists 20–3 reveal the antithetical nature of ἐγραμμάτευε by chiasmus:

20, 1f. *h*ε͂]ι Θ[οινίλος ....] Ἀχαρ[νε]ὺς ἐγραμμάτευε *h*ελ[λε̄νο]τ[αμίας ε͂̓ν ....].[.......... ἐκ Κεραμ]έο̄ν
21, 1f. *h*ε͂ι Προ̄τόνι]κος ἐκ Κεραμέο̄ν Ἐπιχάρος [ἐγραμμάτευε *h*ελλε̄νοταμίας ε͂̓ν .....μ]αχος Χαριδέμο Χσυπεταίο̄ν
22, 2ff. *h*ε͂ι] Φιλε[..........]εκτο[.......... ἐγραμ[μάτευε *h*ελ]λε̄νοτ[αμίας ε͂̓ν Δι]ονύσιος
23, 3ff. *h*ε͂[ι ..]μοχάρε̄ς Μυρ[ρ]ιν[όσι]ος ἐγραμμά[τ]ευε [*h*ε]λλε̄νο-ταμίας ε͂̓ν [Φι]λέταιρος [Ἰ]κα[ριεύ]ς

The prescripts of lists 16, 17 and 19 are illegible, and list 18 is lost altogether, so that we do not know exactly when, between list 15 and list 20, the composer of the record chose to adopt chiastic order; but once adopted, the new formula was maintained until in list 25 (24 is missing) the character of the whole prescript was altered by naming all the members of the board.

The serious problem lies in lists 11 and 12:

11, 1 *h*ἒι Στρόμ[βιχος Χο]λλείδἑς ἐγ[ραμ]μάτευε
12, 1 *h*ἒι [Σ]οφίας ἐγρα[μμάτ]ευε ᾿Ελευσίνι(ος)

In list 11 the order which I have described as 'antithetical' is adopted; yet there is no antithesis, as no one else is named. List 12 reverts to the earlier practice, in which ἐγραμμάτευε is treated as *C*. The co-secretary and the eponym are not named in the prescript, but separately, at the bottom of the list (12, 36), and they are stated in 'antithetical' order: Σάτυρος Λευκονοεὺς χσυνεγραμ[μάτευε Σ]οφοκλἒς Κολō[νἒθεν *h*ελλἒνοταμί]ας ἒν. The explanation of these phenomena is that formulae belonging to one series of documents influenced similar formulae belonging to other series. In the prescripts of decrees several individuals were named as performing different functions. The composer of the prescript of a tribute-list therefore had available to him three sets of models: (i) previous tribute-lists, (ii) other documents in which only one official was named, (iii) other documents, notably decrees, in which several officials were named and their different functions specified. Lists 11 and 12 are a battle-ground of models, and lists 13ff. represent the victory of the third set of models.

The existence of formulae has an important bearing on the compilation and use of statistics. Suppose, for example, that we wanted statistical information on the relation between the imperatival infinitive and its object in the language of Attic documents. *IG*, 1^2, 81 (421/0 B.C.), 5 opens with the words τὸν ῾Ρετὸν τὸμ παρὰ τõ [ἄ]στεος γεφυρõσαι, and 94 (418/17 B.C.), 4f. with the words ἔρχσαι τὸ *h*ιερὸν τõ Κόδρο . . . καὶ μισθõσαι τὸ τέμενος κατὰ τὰς συνγραφάς. In the former case the object precedes the infinitive, and in the latter it follows. Now suppose that we add to these two examples the scores of decrees which record the public commendation of individuals or states and begin, almost without exception, with the words ἐπαινέσαι τὸν δεῖνα. If we counted each of these commendatory decrees as one example, we should conclude that it was much commoner in Attic decrees for the object to follow the imperatival infinitive than to precede it. In one sense, this is literally true; but it would not necessarily follow that the composer of an Attic decree, if required to say 'strip the statue of its gold', would be more likely to say περιελέσθαι τοῦ ἀγάλματος τὸν χρυσόν than τοῦ ἀγάλματος τὸν χρυσὸν περιελέσθαι. The Athenians often had occasion to commend people; they rarely had occasion to bridge the Rheitus or to fence the sanctuary of Codrus. Therefore the expression of commendation became formulaic at an early date; and the more instances of the use of a formula we include in our statistics, the more we distort the picture which our statistics were intended to give us.[1]

The influence of such formulae on each other may be seen on a grand scale in decrees. An Attic decree usually makes the provision: 'let the Secretary of the Council inscribe this decree on a stone stele'. This provision sometimes begins with the words τὸ δὲ ψήφισμα τόδε, sometimes with ἀναγράψαι δέ, sometimes with τὸν δὲ γραμματέα; by the end of the fourth century the form beginning with ἀναγράψαι δέ emerges, after a varied career, with the status of a formula. Another common provision is 'and invite the ambassadors (etc.) to dinner in the prytaneum'; and here too the formulation beginning with καλέσαι δέ or καὶ καλέσαι has an almost unchallenged predominance.[2] To draw general syntactical conclusions from these instances would be not only rash in principle but in conflict with the results of statistical inference from contemporary literature. If we could trace a formula back to its source we should find that the initial lead of one formulation over its alternatives was the product of what we, as students of the history of the language, would be compelled to call 'chance'. Once the lead is established, the likelihood that this leading formulation will become a formula is greatly increased; so is the likelihood that it will help to determine the

[1] Schwyzer, II, p. 693, by going on from a distinction between 'habituell' and 'okkasionell' to cite many examples of the type Κεκροπὶς ἐπρυτάνευε and add 'Doch liest man auch ἔγνω δᾶμος Del.[3] 623 (Erythrae, II[a])', may give the impression that Κεκροπὶς ἐπρυτάνευε exemplifies a general principle while ἔγνω δᾶμος demands a special explanation. This impression would be fundamentally misleading, since the alternative formulations are syntactically indifferent and the predominance of either in a given community is a question of habit and tradition.

[2] McDonald, pp. 153f.

predominant formulation of other utterances of similar structure and content. When these formulations conform to each other, their very conformity strengthens the predominance of the formula with which the process began.

Despite this, certain formulae have been used statistically to prove that one syntactical order is 'normal' and others 'abnormal'. But to collect hundreds of instances of dedicatory inscriptions or artists' signatures[1] or proverbs,[2] and to argue syntactically from them, is illegitimate. The more instances we collect of identical formulation of a single type of utterance, the more conclusively do we demonstrate the existence of a formula and the less relevant does our information become to the establishment of general syntactical rules. Two utterances of type (*a*) tend to be formulated similarly simply because they are both (*a*).

Every sustained utterance, colloquial or literary or administrative, is necessarily in some degree formulaic; it is hard to say anything which does not in some way resemble something which one has said or heard before. I set out below the various ways in which Homer, in the catalogue of ships, and Herodotus inform us of the name of the commander of a force or ship.[3] I arrange the examples in an order designed to show (so far as is possible when one is compelled to operate in only two dimensions) the extent to which each example is derivative or original. Dots indicate words in apposition to the commander's name, dashes words in apposition to the name of the force.

(*a*) B 727 ἀλλὰ Μέδων κόσμησε ...
(*b*) B 704 ἀλλά σφεας κόσμησε Ποδάρκης ...
I, 103, 3 ἦγε δὲ αὐτοὺς ... Μαδύης ...
VI, 92, 2 ἦγε δὲ αὐτοὺς ... Εὐρυβάτης ...
IX, 17, 2 ἦγε δὲ αὐτοὺς Ἁρμοκύδης ...
VII, 63 ἦρχε δέ σφεων Ὀτάσπης ...
VI, 103, 1 ἦγον δέ σφεας στρατηγοὶ δέκα
VII, 222 ἐστρατήγεε δὲ αὐτῶν Δημόφιλος ...
IX, 28, 6 ἐστρατήγεε δὲ αὐτῶν Ἀριστείδης ...
IX, 96, 2 ἐστρατήγεε δὲ αὐτοῦ Τιγράνης ...

[1] Wackernagel, *Gesetz*, pp. 430ff.
[2] Fischer, pp. 2ff., Barth, pp. 28f., 45f.
[3] I exclude such passages as Hdt. VII, 215, IX, 66, 2, where the relative τῶν means not καὶ τούτων but τούτους ὧν.

VIII, 131, 2 στρατηγὸς δὲ καὶ ναύαρχος ἦν Λευτυχίδης ...
VII, 121, 3 στρατηγοὺς δὲ παρείχετο Σμερδομένεά τε καὶ Μεγάβυζον[1]
VII, 71 ἄρχοντα δὲ παρείχοντο Μασσάγην ...[1]
VII, 61, 2 καὶ ἄρχοντα παρείχοντο Ὀτανέα ...
VII, 62, 2 ἡγεμόνα παρεχόμενοι Μεγάπανον ...
VII, 67, 1 ἡγεμόνα παρεχόμενοι Ἀριόμαρδον ...
(*c*) B 609 τῶν ἦρχ' ... Ἀγαπήνωρ ἑξήκοντα νεῶν
B 736 τῶν ἦρχ' Εὐρύπυλος ...
B 826 τῶν ἦρχε ... Πάνδαρος
B 512 τῶν ἦρχ' Ἀσκάλαφος καὶ Ἰάλμενος ...
B 830 τῶν ἦρχ' Ἄδρηστός τε καὶ Ἄμφιος ...
B 842 τῶν ἦρχ' Ἱππόθοός τε Πύλαιός τ' ...
IV, 120, 3 τῆς ἦρχε Ἰδάνθυρσος
IV, 128, 2 τῆς ἦρχε Σκώπασις[2]
VII, 211, 1 τῆς ἦρχε Ὑδάρνης
VII, 180 τῆς ἦρχε Πρηξῖνος
VIII, 47 τῆς ἦρχε ... Φάϋλλος
VIII, 82, 1 τῆς ἦρχε ... Παναίτιος ...
VII, 181, 1 τῆς ἐτριηράρχεε Ἀσωνίδης
VII, 182 τῆς ἐτριηράρχεε Φόρμος ...
VII, 121, 3 τῆς ἐστρατήγεον Τριτανταίχμης τε καὶ Γέργις
VII, 194, 1 τῶν ἐστρατήγεε ... Σανδώκης
VII, 205, 2 τῶν ἐστρατήγεε Λεοντιάδης ...
B 713 τῶν ἦρχ' ... ἕνδεκα νηῶν Εὔμηλος
B 586 τῶν οἱ ... ἦρχε ... Μενέλαος ἑξήκοντα νεῶν
B 576 τῶν ἑκατὸν νηῶν ἦρχε ... Ἀγαμέμνων ...
(*d*) V, 1, 1 τῶν ὁ Μεγάβαζος ἦρχε[2]
VII, 233, 1 τῶν ὁ Λεοντιάδης ἐστρατήγεε[2]
(*e*) B 685 τῶν αὖ πεντήκοντα νεῶν ἦν ἀρχὸς Ἀχιλλεύς
B 731 τῶν αὖθ' ἡγείσθην ... Ποδαλείριος ἠδὲ Μαχάων
B 540 τῶν αὖθ' ἡγεμόνευ' Ἐλεφήνωρ ...
B 552 τῶν αὖθ' ἡγεμόνευε ... Μενεσθεύς
B 563 τῶν αὖθ' ἡγεμόνευε ... Διομήδης καὶ Σθένελος ...

[1] Here there is explicit antithesis between the command of a force and some other aspect of it.

[2] I doubt the propriety of including these three passages in my list, since in all three cases (note the definite article in two of them) the purpose of the relative clause is not so much to inform us who the commander was as to remind us which force is being referred to.

	B 601	τῶν αὖθ' ἡγεμόνευε . . . Νέστωρ
	B 627	τῶν αὖθ' ἡγεμόνευε Μέγης . . .
	B 740	τῶν αὖθ' ἡγεμόνευε . . . Πολυποίτης . . .
	B 837	τῶν αὖθ' . . . ἦρχ' Ἄσιος . . .
	B 622	τῶν δ' . . . ἦρχε . . . Διώρης[1]
(*f*)	B 718	τῶν δὲ Φιλοκτήτης ἦρχεν . . . ἑπτὰ νεῶν
	B 636	τῶν μὲν Ὀδυσσεὺς ἦρχε . . .
	B 758	τῶν μὲν Πρόθοος . . . ἡγεμόνευε
	B 657	τῶν μὲν Τληπόλεμος . . . ἡγεμόνευε
	B 698	τῶν αὖ Πρωτεσίλαος . . . ἡγεμόνευε
	B 650	τῶν μὲν ἄρ' Ἰδομενεὺς . . . ἡγεμόνευε Μηριόνης τ' . . .
	B 620	τῶν μὲν ἄρ' Ἀμφίμαχος καὶ Θάλπιος ἡγησάσθην[1]
	B 870	τῶν μὲν ἄρ' Ἀμφίμαχος καὶ Νάστης ἡγησάσθην
	B 678	τῶν αὖ Φείδιππός τε καὶ Ἄντιφος ἡγησάσθην
(*g*)	B 623	τῶν δὲ τετάρτων ἦρχε Πολύξεινος . . .[1]
	VI, 111, 1	τοῦ μὲν δεξιοῦ κέρεος ἡγέετο . . . Καλλίμαχος[1]
	VII, 97	τῆς δὲ ἄλλης στρατιῆς ἐστρατήγεον οἱ δύο
	VII, 97	τοῦ δὲ ναυτικοῦ ἐστρατήγεον οἵδε[2]
(*h*)	VII, 66, 2	τούτων δὲ ἦρχον οἵδε[2]
	VII, 68	τούτων δὲ ἦρχον οἵδε[2]
	VII, 73	τούτων συναμφοτέρων ἦρχε Ἀρτόχμης . . .
	VII, 77	τούτων πάντων ἦρχε Βάδρης . . .
	VII, 80	τούτων δὲ τῶν νησιωτέων ἦρχε Μαρδόντης . . .
	VII, 81	τούτου ὦν τοῦ στρατοῦ ἦρχον μὲν οὗτοι . . .[3]
	VII, 121, 3	ταύτης μὲν δὴ ἐστρατήγεον Μαρδόνιός τε καὶ Μασίστης[1]
	VII, 83, 1	τῶν δὲ μυρίων τούτων --- ἐστρατήγεε μὲν Ὑδάρνης[3]
(*i*)	VII, 79	τούτων δὲ Μασίστιος . . . ἦρχε
(*j*)	VII, 82, 2	ἐστρατήγεον δὲ τούτων --- Μαρδόνιός τε . . . καὶ Τριτανταίχμης[3]
(*k*)	VII, 173, 2	ἐστρατήγεε δὲ Λακεδαιμονίων μὲν Εὐαίνετος[1]
(*l*)	B 858	Μυσῶν δὲ Χρόμις ἦρχε καὶ Ἔννομος . . .
	B 645	Κρητῶν δ' Ἰδομενεὺς . . . ἡγεμόνευε

[1] Here there is explicit antithesis (with μέν/δέ), within a single complex sentence, between different forces.

[2] Followed by a list of names.

[3] Here there is explicit antithesis between the command of a force and some other aspect of it.

B 863 Μῄοσιν αὖ Μέσθλης τε καὶ Ἄντιφος ἡγησάσθην...
B 494 Βοιωτῶν μὲν Πηνελέως καὶ Λήϊτος ἦρχον
VII, 72, 2 Παφλαγόνων μέν νυν καὶ Ματιηνῶν Δῶτος... ἦρχε[1]
B 517 αὐτὰρ Φωκήων Σχέδιος καὶ Ἐπίστροφος ἦρχον
B 856 αὐτὰρ Ἁλιζώνων Ὀδίος καὶ Ἐπίστροφος ἦρχον
(*m*) B 844 αὐτὰρ Θρήϊκας ἦγ' Ἀκάμας καὶ Πείροος ...
B 756 Μαγνήτων δ' ἦρχε Πρόθοος
VII, 62, 2 Κισσίων δὲ ἦρχε Ἀνάφης ...
VII, 66, 1 Ἀρίων δὲ ἦρχε Σισάμνης ...
VII, 67, 1 Σαραγγέων δὲ ἦρχε Φερενδάτης ...
VII, 75, 2 Θρηίκων δὲ --- ἦρχε Βασσάκης ...
VII, 64, 2 Βακτρίων δὲ καὶ Σακέων ἦρχε Ὑστάσπης ...
VII, 69, 2 Ἀραβίων δὲ καὶ Αἰθιόπων --- ἦρχε Ἀρσάμης ...
VII, 74, 2 Λυδῶν δὲ καὶ Μυσῶν ἦρχε Ἀρταφρένης ...
VII, 79 Μαρῶν δὲ καὶ Κόλχων ἦρχε Φαρανδάτης ...
VII, 97 Αἰγυπτίων δὲ ἐστρατήγεε Ἀχαιμένης ...
VIII, 131, 3 Ἀθηναίων δὲ ἐστρατήγεε Ξάνθιππος ...
B 638 Αἰτωλῶν δ' ἡγεῖτο Θόας ...
B 851 Παφλαγόνων δ' ἡγεῖτο Πυλαιμένεος λάσιον κῆρ
B 527 Λοκρῶν δ' ἡγεμόνευεν ... Αἴας
B 819 Δαρδανίων αὖτ' ἦρχεν ... Αἰνείας
B 816 Τρωσὶ μὲν ἡγεμόνευε ... Ἕκτωρ
VII, 69, 2 τῶν μὲν δὴ ὑπὲρ Αἰγύπτου Αἰθιόπων καὶ Ἀραβίων ἦρχε Ἀρσάμης[1]
VII, 62, 1 οἱ δὲ Μῆδοι ἄρχοντα μὲν παρείχοντο Τιγράνην ...[2]
VII, 67, 2 Πάκτυες δὲ ἄρχοντα παρείχοντο Ἀρταΰντην ...
(*n*) B 862 Φόρκυς αὖ Φρύγας ἦγε καὶ Ἀσκάνιος ...
B 557 Αἴας δ' ἐκ Σαλαμῖνος ἄγεν δυοκαίδεκα νῆας
B 748 Γουνεὺς δ' ἐκ Κύφου ἦγε δύω καὶ εἴκοσι νῆας
B 671 Νιρεὺς αὖ Σύμηθεν ἄγε τρεῖς νῆας ἐΐσας
B 653 Τληπόλεμος δ' ... ἐκ Ῥόδου ἐννέα νῆας ἄγεν
B 867 Νάστης αὖ Καρῶν ἡγήσατο ---

[1] Here there is explicit antithesis (with μέν/δέ), within a single complex sentence, between different forces.

[2] Here there is explicit antithesis between the command of a force and some other aspect of it.

(*o*) B 631 αὐτὰρ Ὀδυσσεὺς ἦγε Κεφαλλῆνας ---
B 848 αὐτὰρ Πυραίχμης ἄγε Παίονας ---
B 840 Ἱππόθοος δ' ἄγε φῦλα Πελασγῶν ---
B 876 Σαρπηδὼν δ' ἦρχεν Λυκίων καὶ Γλαῦκος ...

A first glance over this list may suggest unlimited variety of formulation, but a second glance corrects the impression. Homer and Herodotus confine themselves to a proportion of the possible total of permutations.[1] If we turn from information on the commanders of troops to information on the names of persons and places, we find that Herodotus's formulations of 'whose name was ...' in part correspond to his formulations of 'commanded by'; οὔνομα δέ οἱ ἦν *N* ~ ἦγε δ' αὐτοὺς ὁ δεῖνα and τοῦ οὔνομά ἐστι *N* ~ τῶν ἦρχε ὁ δεῖνα. Yet straightway we encounter a new formulation: I, 179, 4 Ἶς οὔνομα αὐτῇ, I, 205, 1 Τόμυρίς οἱ ἦν οὔνομα, II, 29, 3 Ταχομψὼ οὔνομα αὐτῇ ἐστι, VIII, 32, 1 Τιθορέα οὔνομα αὐτῇ. This has no counterpart among the formulations of 'whose commander was ...'; but if we seek its ancestry, we may find a clue in Hecataeus, fr. 282 ἐν δ' αὐτοῖσι πόλις, Παρικάνη οὔνομα.

This brings us back finally to the 'conflict of pattern and principle' of which I spoke in ch. I, (ii). In attempting to explain the word order in any given Greek utterance, we must ask not only 'with what principles is it consistent?' but also 'what are its models and what is the history of its models?'[2] The part played by patterns and models offers an explanation of the process by which the syntactical

[1] It should be remembered that the Homeric catalogue, unlike Hdt. VII, is simultaneously a catalogue of forces and a catalogue of heroes.

[2] Barth, pp. 37ff., emphasises the importance of formal analogy and association. Frisk, p. 76, makes the point that an order originally determined logically may become 'mechanisiert' through familiarity and may eventually be employed in utterances to which the original determinants are entirely inapplicable. Elsewhere in his argument he perhaps underestimates the importance of this phenomenon. Thus (pp. 56ff.) he explains the order *P S* in τῶν ἦρχε ὁ δεῖνα by saying that ἦρχε is a 'Rubrikwort', and the exceptions X. *An.* I, 7, 11 ὧν Ἀρταγέρσης ἦρχε, *HG*, III, 1, 6, IV, 8, 10, VI, 5, 11, by saying (p. 59) that for Xenophon (unlike Herodotus and Thucydides) ἦρχε is *not* a 'Rubrikwort'. What then is the explanation of X. *An.* IV, 8, 18 ὧν ἦρχεν Αἰσχίνης ὁ Ἀκαρνάν, *ibid.* ὧν ἦρχε Κλεάνωρ ὁ Ὀρχομένιος, *HG*, I, 2, 16? It might seem that ἦρχε cannot both be and not be a 'Rubrikwort' for the same author in the same works. But perhaps it can, provided that we reverse the cause and effect. Herodotus chooses to *make* ἦρχε a 'Rubrikwort' by putting it first; Xenophon sometimes chooses to do so, and sometimes not; but the word order cannot be invoked to explain the choice.

principles, secondary in character, came in course of time to supersede primary logical principles. It may be said that from the first the scales were weighted in favour of SV and OV by four phenomena:

(i) Demonstratives as a whole tended to be treated as M^a and constituted a high proportion of the commoner M^a. Many demonstratives are pronouns and may therefore be S or O; but no demonstratives are V. Thus $|S(=M^a)\ V$ and $|O(=M^a)\ V$ served as models determining $|S(=M^b)\ V$ and $|O(=M^b)\ V$, without serious competition from $|V(=M^a)\ S$ or $|V(=M^a)\ O$.

(ii) When $S=C$, it is often adequately expressed by the person-index of V, but whereas the case-index of a noun or pronoun may express its relationship to V no part of a noun or pronoun expresses the content of V. Therefore $|S(=N)\ V(=C)$ was always necessarily commoner than $|V(=N)\ S(=C)$, and served as a model determining $|S(=N)\ V(=N)$.[1]

(iii) The copula is the only V which I have consistently symbolised as M^q; but the number of V which may in varying degrees have the character of the copula is large, and these V constituted a productive model for $|N\ C(=V)$ in general.[2]

(iv) When the same utterance may be formulated either as $|S(=N)\ V(=C)$ or as $|V(=N)\ S(=N)$, the tendencies just described determined a preference for the former. This in turn served as an additional model determining $|S(=N)\ V(=N)$.[3]

[1] Cf. Ammann, *Unt.* I, pp. 20f., Kaibel, pp. 99f.

[2] Cf. Rass, pp. 33ff.

[3] It may be the case that a single action or passion with multiple agents is commoner in life than multiple action by a single agent, so that

$$N(=S_1)\ C(=V)+N(=S_2)$$

describes a commoner state of affairs than $N(=V_1)\ C(=S)+N(=V_2)$; but I would feel uneasy in dealing with so high a level of generalisation.

CHAPTER V

STYLE

What purports to be an account of the 'style' of a Greek author often constitutes what might more reasonably be regarded as an account of his 'language'; at any rate, if one were asked to give an account of the author's 'language'—that is to say, *the author's* language as opposed to the common factors of the language of the nation to which he belongs—the result might not differ in kind from what is presented as an account of his 'style'.

I do not infer from this that 'style' is an illusion, a term which has no useful application; nor do I infer that 'style' is a genus of which 'language' is one species, the other species being the author's selection, treatment and arrangement of his material. It is rather that style is an epiphenomenon of language, a group of aspects of language. Suppose, for example, that an author uses δεῖ twice as often as χρή. That is simply a linguistic fact. Suppose that another author, a compatriot and contemporary of the first, uses χρή twice as often as δεῖ. That is another linguistic fact. But put the two linguistic facts together, and by virtue of mere juxtaposition they are suddenly transformed into stylistic facts. Of the two authors, one has chosen differently from the other; and as soon as the possibility of choice is seen to exist, we can begin to speak of style. Or again: suppose that the first author concentrates all his instances of χρή in the first third of his work, while in the second author's work χρή and δεῖ are evenly distributed. These are stylistic facts, which are out of place in an account of the authors' *language*.

In making a choice, an author can be ahead of his time or behind it; he can anticipate a development which will become general in the next generation, or ignore a development well established in the previous generation. The fact that Thucydides describes the despondency of the Athenians retreating from Syracuse as κατήφεια (VII, 75, 5), taken by itself, is of no stylistic significance; it acquires such significance when we learn that Homer uses this noun and that between Homer and Thucydides no other extant author uses it.

Since the element of choice in word order is so large, it is a particularly suitable subject for stylistic enquiry. It might even prove that authors could be more clearly differentiated, the chronological developments of an author's style more clearly illuminated, and the spurious intrusions into the corpus of his work more clearly identified, by means of this study than by any other aspect of form whatsoever. We have to ask, in respect of word order, as in any other respect, not only 'what choice does the author make?' but also 'how many times running does he make the same choice?' The answer to the first question is a linguistic fact, which becomes a stylistic fact when it is related to the answers to the same question asked of other authors. The second question is not a linguistic question at all, and the answer to it is wholly, from the very beginning, stylistic.[1]

Let us reconsider, from this point of view, Hdt. II, 26, 2. In ch. IV, B, (i) our purpose was to discover the answer to the linguistic question 'what is the relation, in respect of order, between *C* and *N*?' Now the question is different: 'what degree of consistency in the treatment of *C* and *N* does Herodotus pursue?' It is obvious that he pursues, and achieves, morphological and syntactical variety by giving the syntactical predicate, which is *C* throughout from καὶ τοῦ οὐρανοῦ to ταύτῃ δὲ ὁ βορέης, the forms ἑστᾶσι and ἕστηκε in the τῇ μέν / τῇ δέ clauses, changing it to ἦν ἡ στάσις in the ταύτῃ μέν clause, and omitting it altogether in the clause ταύτῃ δὲ ὁ βορέης. The co-ordinated *N* in the complex protasis are continuous in ὁ βορέης τε καὶ ὁ χειμών, separated in τοῦ νότου...καὶ τῆς μεσαμβρίης, and when the north wind is referred to in the apodosis the order is reversed: ὑπὸ τοῦ χειμῶνος καὶ τοῦ βορέω. νῦν precedes the syntactical subject in τῇ μὲν νῦν ὁ βορέης... but follows it in τῇ δὲ ὁ νότος νῦν.... The *C* ἔρχεται is the last element in the clause κατάπερ νῦν τῆς Λιβύης ἔρχεται, but the *C* ἐργάζεται is 'sandwiched' in the clause τάπερ νῦν ἐργάζεται τὸν Νεῖλον. We have the impression that from a stylistic rather than a linguistic point of view one of the most powerful determinants of order in Herodotus is the desire to achieve variety so far as this is consistent with the prin-

[1] Schwyzer, II, p. 697, gives the impression that 'okkasionell' order is a 'Stilmittel', while 'habituell' order is not; so too Leumann, pp. 794ff., treats hyperbaton under 'Stilistik', not under 'Wortstellung', despite the occurrence of hyperbaton in non-literary prose (cf. Chantraine, pp. 79f.). This allocation of selected phenomena of order to the category 'Style' reminds one of a modern Trimalchio's description of his house: 'It's been built, but the architecture ain't put on yet.'

ciples shared by him with other Greek writers and the stock of models available to him.

The effects of this pursuit of variety are often forced upon our attention more obtrusively than in Herodotus. Here are the opening words of sections of the Hippocratic *De Carne*:

5, 1	τὰ δὲ σπλάγχνα ὧδέ μοι δοκεῖ ξυστῆναι
7	ὁ δὲ πνεύμων πρὸς τῇ καρδίῃ ἐγένετο ὧδε
8	τὸ δὲ ἧπαρ ὧδε ξυνέστη
9	ὁ δὲ σπλὴν ξυνέστη ὧδε
10	τὰ δὲ ἄρθρα ὧδε ἐγένετο
12, 1	οἱ δὲ ὀδόντες ὕστερον γίνονται διὰ τόδε
14	αἱ δὲ τρίχες φύονται ὧδε
15, 1	ἀκούει δὲ διὰ τόδε
16, 1	ὀσφραίνεται δ' ὁ ἐγκέφαλος ὑγρὸς ἐών
17, 1	ὁρῇ δὲ διὰ τοῦτο
18, 1	διαλέγεται δὲ [διὰ] τὸ πνεῦμα ἕλκων

Deliberate variety of order is as obvious here as variety of vocabulary; in other words, the proximity of ὧδε ξυνέστη is among the determinants of ξυνέστη ὧδε.

It appears from the history of other Indo-European languages that syntactical principles of order have a greater endurance than logical principles, and I have suggested that in Greek itself the primary logical principles 'weighted the scales' in favour of an increasing dominance by syntactical patterns of order. If the Greeks had not possessed so intense a degree of artistic self-consciousness, it may be thought likely that syntactical patterns would have established themselves much earlier and much more firmly.[1] We find in fact that in the language of the New Testament rules of order are much more easily defined in syntactical terms than they are in Classical Greek.[2] It appears that Greek literature, by attaching value to variety of form, maintained a resistance to that drift towards syntactical uniformity which has been the fate of other languages, and that pagan post-Classical literature diverged increasingly from the colloquial language of its own day by reasserting the primacy of logical rules of order.

[1] Barth, p. 26, seems to imply—rightly, I think—that it was conscious art which maintained the elasticity of Greek word order for so long.

[2] Cf. Barth, p. 48, Wundt, p. 369, on the part played by colloquial language in enforcing formal analogy.

INDEX OF PASSAGES

I. INSCRIPTIONS

II. LITERATURE